I0606160

WOMEN IN POETRY

Elizabeth Barrett Browning

The inspiration for the cover illustration
by Lou Benesch is from
'The Romance of the Swan's Nest':

Little Ellie sits alone,
And the smile she softly uses
Fills the silence like a speech,
While she thinks what shall be done,
And the sweetest pleasure chooses
For her future within reach.

Little Ellie in her smile
Chooses – I will have a lover
Riding on a steed of steeds:
He shall love me without guile,
And to him I will discover
The swan's nest among the reeds.

WOMEN IN POETRY

Elizabeth Barrett Browning

Introduction by Pelé Cox

G:

Published in 2026
by Gemini Gift Books
Part of Gemini Books Group

Based in Woodbridge and London

Marine House, Tide Mill Way,
Woodbridge, Suffolk IP12 1AP
United Kingdom

www.geminibooks.com

Poetry by Elizabeth Barrett Browning
Introduction and critiques by Pelé Cox
Cover illustration by Lou Benesch
Poems collated by Becky Freeth

ISBN 978-1-78675-212-3

A CIP catalogue record for this book is available from the British Library.

Manufacturer's EU Representative: Eurolink Compliance Limited,
25 Herbert Place, Dublin, D02 AY86, Republic of Ireland.
admin@eurolink-europe.ie

Printed in China

10 9 8 7 6 5 4 3 2 1

Contents

Introduction 6

Chapter One: Love 12
Chapter Two: Death & Spirituality 46
Chapter Three: Social Justice 96
Chapter Four: Women's Rights & Feminism 124

Acknowledgements 160

Introduction

"The works of women are symbolical; we sew, sew, prick our fingers, and dull our sight, producing what? A pair of slippers?"

Aurora Leigh, Book One

Elizabeth Barrett Browning (known as EBB) remains one of the literary giants of the nineteenth century, not only for groundbreaking political poetry, such as 'The Runaway Slave at Pilgrim's Point' – one of the great abolitionist poems of the age – and for some of the most beautiful love poems ever written, but also for a remarkable life, much of it conducted from a sickbed.

Her pioneering poems on gender politics, the anti-slavery movement and the Italian Risorgimento almost won her the crown of the first female poet laureate, which was lost, instead, to Alfred, Lord Tennyson. Hers is a story in two halves. First, she endured a mysterious debilitating illness, which doctors failed to diagnose, followed by, at the age of twenty-two, the loss of her mother, then her two brothers within six months of each other. Nonetheless, a constant poetic output brought her acclaim and enticed her nine-years-younger future husband, the poet Robert Browning, with whom she spent the second half of her life. At forty-one she emigrated to her beloved Italy, which Lord Byron and Percy Bysshe Shelley had called the "paradise of exiles". She would never see her father again.

"Who so loves believes the impossible," she had said. She gave birth to her first child "Pen" at the age of forty-two, her health recovering greatly. What united these profoundly diverse stages in her life was her writing and study of poetry. Even the pain and grief she suffered did not stop her from developing one of the most progressive female voices in poetic history, or from becoming a scholar of the highest order. Homer, Shelley, Byron, Horace were more like friends to her.

Her epic poem *Aurora Leigh*, in nine books, is a novel in verse (a *roman-à-clef,* or *bildungsroman)* and was a bestseller of the time; the story in poetry of a young woman training herself to be a true poet. She claimed it to be "the most mature of my works and the one into which my highest conviction of life and art have entered." Aurora Leigh develops her insight and intellect against all odds, reading the classics while she experiences the trials and tribulations of a poet's life. Her lines "[I] will write my story / for my better self" describe a woman writing a poem about a woman writing a poem.

Born on 6 March 1806, in County Durham, England, Elizabeth Barrett was the eldest of twelve children from a wealthy family of slave owners. An early exposure to literature, and a natural vocation for it, led her to begin composing poetry at a young age. By eleven, she had already produced a substantial collection, much of which survives.

Tragically, at fifteen, after falling from her horse, she began suffering from intense spinal pain and then respiratory issues, possibly tuberculosis. These health challenges confined her to her home and, to manage the pain, she resorted to laudanum, a powerful opiate, which likely contributed to her frail health. She could only walk with a cane and often used a wheelchair.

Her 1844 collection, called simply *Poems*, solidified her reputation and brought her international renown. This collection showcased her innovative blend of ethical themes couched in conversational language that appealed to a burgeoning mass audience.

She was also a great classicist, and the same frailty that confined her to bed allowed her to nourish her remarkable scholarship and intellect. Yet, bedbound she remained. As with all committed poets, her internal life often composed real-life events. It is said that the figure of Robert Browning, who wrote to her after reading her poetry, reminded her of her baby brother "Bro", whom she adored and who drowned at sea.

After marrying in 1846, a great garden of poetry blossomed, as is evident in her forty-four love sonnets to her husband, the last in which she writes:

> Beloved, thou hast brought me many flowers
> Plucked in the garden, all the summer through
> And winter, and it seemed as if they grew
> In this close room.

Barrett Browning had gained a partner of equal measure who appreciated her intellect and creativity. Her subsequent move to Italy with her husband meant an escape from societal constraints and the rigid expectations placed on women of her time. In Italy, she found not only a new home but also a renewed sense of freedom and inspiration. Her health improved, and it was then that she wrote her most famous poems *Aurora Leigh*, 'Casa Guidi Windows' and *Sonnets from the Portuguese*.

The poems serve as a powerful commentary on women's roles in society and they challenge the traditional notions of femininity. Throughout her work, the poet articulates her belief in the importance of self-determination and liberty. Her influence extended beyond her immediate circle of contemporary writers, reaching even the Americans Emily Dickinson, Edna St. Vincent Millay and, closer to home,

Virginia Woolf and Oscar Wilde, with whom she shares the title of a work 'De Profundis'.

As with George Sand, an admired feminist, her contemporary and muse in the sonnet 'George Sand: A Desire,' the complexities of Barrett Browning's character and her writing reflected the dualities of her experience – late to marriage, she was both a celebrated poet and an invalid; a devoted wife, mother, an independent thinker, an "exile" at the forefront of political change. Her resilience in the face of physical and emotional challenges shaped her poetry of social justice; hers is a body of work that speaks for universal themes of love, loss and the search for identity.

Her long-form use of the traditional ballad was particularly inspiring to Christina Rossetti in that poet's *Goblin Market*. Robert Browning compared Elizabeth's *Sonnets from the Portuguese* to Shakespeare's sonnets. To the later Victorians, she was a jewel in the crown of English poetry, her influence evident in the works of William Morris and Algernon Charles Swinburne. Throughout her life, her determination to carve out a space for herself in a male-dominated literary landscape left an indelible mark on poetry and feminist thought: 'The Runaway Slave at Pilgrim's Point' was inspiration for Toni Morrison's Pulitzer Prize-winning 'Beloved'. Her journey from a frail bedbound lover of poems to a celebrated literary figure symbolizes the potential for transformation and liberation, regardless of societal, or physical, constraints.

She died at the age of fifty-five on 19 June 1861, in Florence, fittingly in the arms of her husband. Her legacy continues to inspire future generations, as her works remain relevant in discussions surrounding gender, art and the complexities of the human experience.

Chapter One: Love

Poems about familial love, friendship and romance span longing as well as loss, but her most poignant and enduring are to husband Robert Browning.

As a woman who spent much of her adolescence in solitude, Barrett Browning's early work expresses a pining for love. By the time she met Robert Browning – about whom she penned her most famous romantic collection, *Sonnets for the Portuguese* – the poet had all but given up on traditional love, expressing in 'Sonnet I' the power with which it pulled her back from the brink of death.

By Victorian standards, Elizabeth was a spinster and distinctly in the minority when she married late in life. Her infatuation with fellow poet, Robert, and her overwhelming delight at finding love defined her mid-century work. From the couple's secret elopement to their "great escape" to Italy (fearing her father's disapproval of the marriage), Elizabeth's later years played out like the romantic fantasies that she poured onto the page in timeless scriptures such as 'Sonnet XLIII', which is among the greatest romantic dedications of all time.

Despite her devotion to Robert, her art also showed that she was sceptical about men's love and commitment. 'A Man's Requirements' suggests she was holding something back, cautious that falling too deeply could also cause great pain, not to mention her fear of losing anyone else she loved.

After all, her life was deeply afflicted by loss: she lost an infant sister in 1814, her mother in 1828, then in 1840, two of her brothers, Edward and Samuel, died unexpectedly, in quick succession. Poems such as 'Grief' were a more sorrowful reflection on love. Others like 'The Pet-Name', about her family nickname "Ba", display a yearning for the happy and secure childhood that "sweet memories left behind".

Love

We cannot live, except thus mutually
We alternate, aware or unaware,
The reflex act of life: and when we bear
Our virtue onward most impulsively,
Most full of invocation, and to be
Most instantly compellant, certes, there
We live most life, whoever breathes most air
And counts his dying years by sun and sea.
But when a soul, by choice and conscience, doth
Throw out her full force on another soul,
The conscience and the concentration both make
mere life, Love. For Life in perfect whole
And aim consummated, is Love in sooth,
As nature's magnet – heat rounds pole with pole.

✷✷✷ Critique: 'Love'

This sonnet plumbs the essence of love, entwining imagery of the natural world with the march of life to arouse love's dormant power. The sonnet form allows Barrett Browning to build her argument methodically, culminating first in the declaration, "We live most life, whoever breathes most air." Love is oxygen, a grand gulp of existence.

We should not forget that Elizabeth suffered from ulcerative tuberculosis; often weak and her breathing laboured, oxygen was at a conscious premium. Moreover, it was the love of Robert Browning – he was literally "a breath of fresh air" – that had rescued her from a cataleptic existence in Wimpole Street, London.

The opening lines ("We cannot live...") suggest that the lovers amble along in parallel, in balanced reciprocity, until they live life to the full by enacting their love for each other; soul on soul. Love is therefore an intrinsic bond that is first felt and then actioned. "Sun and sea" express also the brightness and calmness of the halcyon future that awaits the lovers.

The more EBB invokes "sun, sea, soul, life, nature", the more she suggests that love is entwined with the very fabric of what is elemental. Verbs animate the concept of love: "breathe, count, concentrate." Love is a great engine, not a static word.

Conspicuous is the number of words beginning with the letter "c", which provide a steady pulse through the poem. The poet conceives of everything in terms of natural forces, alternating, living mutually, then onrushing and outpouring, and finally conjoining. The act of love that ensures union comes in the volta, the turn or shift in thought, of the sonnet: this act of love is to "throw out" the "full force" of the soul on another soul. The soul is feminine: it is "her full force"; it is her soul. The strength of this force can even unite souls that are poles apart and its magnet-heat make opposites attract.

This sonnet is not part of the later *Sonnets from the Portugese*, but it is almost an overture or template for her great poem sequence that is camouflaged as translations. This sonnet is not disguised, but is a direct, standalone message to her newfound love, Robert Browning, with whom she would elope and move to Italy, "For life in perfect whole".

Sonnets from the Portuguese I

I thought once how Theocritus had sung
Of the sweet years, the dear and wished – for years,
Who each one in a gracious hand appears
To bear a gift for mortals, old or young:
And, as I mused it in his antique tongue,
I saw, in gradual vision through my tears,
The sweet, sad years, the melancholy years,
Those of my own life, who by turns had flung
A shadow across me. Straightway I was 'ware,
So weeping, how a mystic Shape did move
Behind me, and drew me backward by the hair;
And a voice said in mastery, while I strove,
"Guess now who holds thee!" "Death," I said, But, there,
The silver answer rang, "Not Death, but Love."

Sonnets from the Portuguese X

Yet, love, mere love, is beautiful indeed
And worthy of acceptation. Fire is bright,
Let temple burn, or flax; an equal light
Leaps in the flame from cedar-plank or weed:
And love is fire. And when I say at need
I love thee ... mark! ... I love thee, in thy sight
I stand transfigured, glorified aright,
With conscience of the new rays that proceed
Out of my face toward thine. There's nothing low
In love, when love the lowest: meanest creatures
Who love God, God accepts while loving so.
And what I feel, across the inferior features
Of what I am, doth flash itself, and show
How that great work of Love enhances Nature's.

Sonnets from the Portuguese XI

And therefore if to love can be desert,
I am not all unworthy. Cheeks as pale
As these you see, and trembling knees that fail
To bear the burden of a heavy heart,
This weary minstrel-life that once was girt
To climb Aornus, and can scarce avail
To pipe now 'gainst the valley nightingale
A melancholy music, why advert
To these things? O Belovèd, it is plain
I am not of thy worth nor for thy place!
And yet, because I love thee, I obtain
From that same love this vindicating grace
To live on still in love, and yet in vain,
To bless thee, yet renounce thee to thy face.

Sonnets from the Portuguese XII

Indeed this very love which is my boast,
And which, when rising up from breast to brow,
Doth crown me with a ruby large enow
To draw men's eyes and prove the inner cost –
This love even, all my worth, to the uttermost,
I should not love withal, unless that thou
Hadst set me an example, shown me how,
When first thine earnest eyes with mine were crossed,
And love called love. And thus, I cannot speak
Of love even, as a good thing of my own:
Thy soul hath snatched up mine all faint and weak,
And placed it by thee on a golden throne –
And that I love (O soul, we must be meek! –)
Is by thee only, whom I love alone.

Sonnets from the Portuguese XIII

And wilt thou have me fashion into speech
The love I bear thee, finding words enough,
And hold the torch out, while the winds are rough,
Between our faces, to cast light upon each?
I drop it at thy feet. I cannot teach
My hand to hold my spirit so far off
From myself, me, that I should bring thee proof,
In words, of love hid in me out of reach.
Nay, let the silence of my womanhood
Commend my woman – love to thy belief,
Seeing that I stand unwon (however wooed)
And rend the garment of my life, in brief,
By a most dauntless, voiceless fortitude,
Lest one touch of this heart convey its grief.

Sonnets from the Portuguese XIV

If thou must love me, let it be for nought
Except for love's sake only. Do not say,
"I love her for her smile – her look – her way
Of speaking gently, – for a trick of thought
That falls in well with mine, and certes brought
A sense of pleasant ease on such a day" –
For these things in themselves, Belovèd, may
Be changed, or change for thee – and love, so wrought,
May be unwrought so. Neither love me for
Thine own dear pity's wiping my cheeks dry:
A creature might forget to weep, who bore
Thy comfort long, and lose thy love thereby!
But love me for love's sake, that evermore
Thou may'st love on, through love's eternity.

Sonnets from the Portuguese XX

Belovèd, my Belovèd, when I think
That thou wast in the world a year ago,
What time I sat alone here in the snow
And saw no footprint, heard the silence sink
No moment at thy voice, but, link by link,
Went counting all my chains as if that so
They never could fall off at any blow
Struck by thy possible hand, why, thus I drink
Of life's great cup of wonder! Wonderful,
Never to feel thee thrill the day or night
With personal act or speech, nor ever cull
Some prescience of thee with the blossoms white
Thou sawest growing! Atheists are as dull,
Who cannot guess God's presence out of sight.

Sonnets from the Portuguese XXI

Say over again, and yet once over again,
That thou dost love me. Though the word repeated
Should seem "a cuckoo – song," as thou dost treat it,
Remember, never to the hill or plain,
Valley and wood, without her cuckoo – strain
Comes the fresh Spring in all her green completed.
Belovèd, I, amid the darkness greeted
By a doubtful spirit-voice, in that doubt's pain
Cry, "Speak once more – thou lovest!" Who can fear
Too many stars, though each in heaven shall roll,
Too many flowers, though each shall crown the year?
Say thou dost love me, love me, love me – toll
The silver iterance! – only minding, Dear,
To love me also in silence with thy soul.

Sonnets from the Portuguese XXIV

Let the world's sharpness like a clasping knife
Shut in upon itself and do no harm
In this close hand of Love, now soft and warm,
And let us hear no sound of human strife
After the click of the shutting. Life to life –
I lean upon thee, Dear, without alarm,
And feel as safe as guarded by a charm
Against the stab of worldlings, who if rife
Are weak to injure. Very whitely still
The lilies of our lives may reassure
Their blossoms from their roots, accessible
Alone to heavenly dews that drop not fewer;
Growing straight, out of man's reach, on the hill.
God only, who made us rich, can make us poor.

Sonnets from the Portuguese XXV

A heavy heart, Belovèd, have I borne
From year to year until I saw thy face,
And sorrow after sorrow took the place
Of all those natural joys as lightly worn
As the stringed pearls, each lifted in its turn
By a beating heart at dance-time. Hopes apace
Were changed to long despairs, till God's own grace
Could scarcely lift above the world forlorn
My heavy heart. Then thou didst bid me bring
And let it drop adown thy calmly great
Deep being! Fast it sinketh, as a thing
Which its own nature does precipitate,
While thine doth close above it, mediating
Betwixt the stars and the unaccomplished fate.

Sonnets from the Portuguese XXVIII

My letters! all dead paper, ... mute and white! –
And yet they seem alive and quivering
Against my tremulous hands which loose the string
And let them drop down on my knee to – night.
This said, ... he wished to have me in his sight
Once, as a friend: this fixed a day in spring
To come and touch my hand ... a simple thing,
Yet I wept for it! – this, ... the paper's light ...
Said, *Dear I love thee*; and I sank and quailed
As if God's future thundered on my past.
This said, *I am thine*, and so its ink has paled
With lying at my heart that beat too fast.
And this ... O Love, thy words have ill availed
If, what this said, I dared repeat at last!

Sonnets from the Portuguese XXIX

I think of thee! – my thoughts do twine and bud
About thee, as wild vines, about a tree,
Put out broad leaves, and soon there's nought to see
Except the straggling green which hides the wood.
Yet, O my palm-tree, be it understood
I will not have my thoughts instead of thee
Who art dearer, better! Rather, instantly
Renew thy presence; as a strong tree should,
Rustle thy boughs and set thy trunk all bare,
And let these bands of greenery which insphere thee,
Drop heavily down, – burst, shattered everywhere!
Because, in this deep joy to see and hear thee
And breathe within thy shadow a new air,
I do not think of thee – I am too near thee.

Sonnets from the Portuguese XLIII

How do I love thee? Let me count the ways.
I love thee to the depth and breadth and height
My soul can reach, when feeling out of sight
For the ends of Being and ideal Grace.
I love thee to the level of everyday's
Most quiet need, by sun and candle-light.
I love thee freely, as men strive for Right;
I love thee purely, as they turn from Praise.
I love thee with the passion put to use
In my old griefs, and with my childhood's faith.
I love thee with a love I seemed to lose
With my lost saints, I love thee with the breath,
Smiles, tears, of all my life! and, if God choose,
I shall but love thee better after death.

✷✷✷ Critique: 'Sonnets from the Portuguese XLIII'

In the small but experimental territory of the sonnet, the poet tends to a world of feeling. This world is both out of reach and close at hand. The speaker is almost washed away by her own emotions. The sonnet form is her own act of creation, giving ground, purpose and momentum to a woman in love.

As if jotted down with the urgency of someone writing equations on a blackboard to find the meaning of love, she maps out love's territory, but is prescriptive and to the point: "I love thee to the depth and breadth and height."

The sonnet is dedicated to her dear "Beloved", as she called Robert, a qualifying and possessive adjective that recurs throughout the collection and which is directed to an idea of daily, free, physical and mental love.

The repetition of the same phrase "I love thee" five times in lines two, five, seven, eight, nine and eleven is not mechanical, like pulling petals from a daisy or counting out a nursery rhyme. Tightly constructed, the poem appears effortless.

This is a love sufficient to itself, more pillow talk than declamation. Their love is interwoven with everyday existence, their every "breath" and vicissitude – "smiles" and "tears". Love encompasses both secular and spiritual existence. On a formal level, it's also important to note the significant deceleration that occurs in the sonnet's penultimate line – "Smiles, tears, of all my life! and, if God choose, I shall but love thee better after death" – are all virtually monosyllables. Elizabeth would die twenty-eight years before her beloved Robert.

A Man's Requirements *(Extract)*

***

Love me in thy gorgeous airs,
When the world has crowned thee;
Love me, kneeling at thy prayers,
With the angels round thee.

Love me pure, as muses do,
Up the woodlands shady:
Love me gaily, fast and true,
As a winsome lady.

Through all hopes that keep us brave,
Farther off or nigher,
Love me for the house and grave, –
And for something higher.

Thus, if thou wilt prove me, Dear,
Woman's love no fable,
I will love *thee* – half a year –
As a man is able.

Pain in Pleasure

A thought ay like a flower upon mine heart,
And drew around it other thoughts like bees
For multitude and thirst of sweetnesses;
Whereat rejoicing, I desired the art
Of the Greek whistler, who to wharf and mart
Could lure those insect swarms from orange-trees
That I might hive with me such thoughts and please
My soul so, always. foolish counterpart
Of a weak man's vain wishes! While I spoke,
The thought I called a flower grew nettle – rough
The thoughts, called bees, stung me to festering:
Oh, entertain (cried Reason as she woke)
Your best and gladdest thoughts but long enough,
And they will all prove sad enough to sting!

A False Step

Sweet, thou hast trod on a heart.
Pass! there's a world full of men;
And women as fair as thou art
Must do such things now and then.

Thou only hast stepped unaware, –
Malice, not one can impute;
And why should a heart have been there
In the way of a fair woman's foot?

It was not a stone that could trip,
Nor was it a thorn that could rend:
Put up thy proud under – lip!
'Twas merely the heart of a friend.

And yet peradventure one day
Thou, sitting alone at the glass,
Remarking the bloom gone away,
Where the smile in its dimplement was,

And seeking around thee in vain
From hundreds who flattered before,
Such a word as, – "Oh, not in the main
Do I hold thee less precious, – but more!"...

Thou 'lt sigh, very like, on thy part: –
"Of all I have known or can know,
I wish I had only that Heart
I trod upon ages ago!"

Change upon Change

Five months ago the stream did flow,
The lilies bloomed within the sedge,
And we were lingering to and fro, –
Where none will track thee in this snow,
Along the stream, beside the hedge.
Ah, Sweet, be free to love and go;
For if I do not hear thy foot,
The frozen river is as mute, –
The flowers have dried down to the root;
And why, since these be changed since May,
Shouldst *thou* change less than *they*?

And slow, slow as the winter snow
The tears have drifted to mine eyes;
And my poor cheeks, five months ago
Set blushing at thy praises so,
Put paleness on for a disguise.

Ah, Sweet, be free to praise and go;
For if my face is turned too pale,
It was thine oath that first did fail, –
It was thy love proved false and frail!
And why, since these be changed, I enow,
Should I change less than *thou*?

Loved Once *(Extract)*

I classed, appraising once,
Earth's lamentable sounds; the welladay,
The jarring yea and nay,
The fall of kisses on unanswering clay,
The sobbed farewell, the welcome mournfuller; –
But all did leaven the air
With a less bitter leaven of sure despair,
Than these words – I loved ONCE.

And who saith, I loved ONCE?
Not angels, whose clear eyes, love, love, foresee,
Love through eternity,
Who, by To Love, do apprehend To Be.
Not God, called LOVE, his noble crown – name, –
casting
A light too broad for blasting!
The great God changing not from everlasting,
Saith never, I loved ONCE.

***

Catarina to Camoens *(Extract)*

***

Will you come? When I'm departed
Where all sweetnesses are hid,
Where thy voice, my tender-hearted,
Will not lift up either lid.
Cry, O lover,
Love is over!
Cry, beneath the cypress green,
"Sweetest eyes were ever seen!"

***

My Heart and I

Enough! we're tired, my heart and I.
We sit beside the headstone thus,
And wish that name were carved for us.
The moss reprints more tenderly
The hard types of the mason's knife,
As heaven's sweet life renews earth's life
With which we're tired, my heart and I.

You see we're tired, my heart and I.
We dealt with books, we trusted men,
And in our own blood drenched the pen,
As if such colours could not fly.
We walked too straight for fortune's end,
We loved too true to keep a friend;
At last we're tired, my heart and I.

How tired we feel, my heart and I!
We seem of no use in the world;
Our fancies hang grey and uncurled
About men's eyes indifferently;
Our voice which thrilled you so, will let
You sleep; our tears are only wet:
What do we here, my heart and I?

So tired, so tired, my heart and I!
It was not thus in that old time
When Ralph sat with me 'neath the lime
To watch the sunset from the sky.
Dear love, you're looking tired, he said;
I, smiling at him, shook my head:
'Tis now we're tired, my heart and I.

So tired, so tired, my heart and I!
Though now none takes me on his arm
To fold me close and kiss me warm
Till each quick breath end in a sigh
Of happy languor. Now, alone,
We lean upon this graveyard stone,
Uncheered, unkissed, my heart and I.

Tired out we are, my heart and I.
Suppose the world brought diadems
To tempt us, crusted with loose gems
Of powers and pleasures? Let it try.
We scarcely care to look at even
A pretty child, or God's blue heaven,
We feel so tired, my heart and I.

Yet who complains? My heart and I?
In this abundant earth no doubt
Is little room for things worn out:
Disdain them, break them, throw them by
And if before the days grew rough
We *once* were loved, used, – well enough,
I think, we've fared, my heart and I.

Grief

I tell you, hopeless grief is passionless;
That only men incredulous of despair,
Half – taught in anguish, through the midnight air
Beat upward to God's throne in loud access
Of shrieking and reproach. Full desertness,
In souls as countries, lieth silent – bare
Under the blanching, vertical eye – glare
Of the absolute Heavens. Deep-hearted man, express
Grief for thy Dead in silence like to death
Most like a monumental statue set
In everlasting watch and moveless woe
Till itself crumble to the dust beneath.
Touch it; the marble eyelids are not wet:
If it could weep, it could arise and go.

Consolation

All are not taken; there are left behind
Living Belovèds, tender looks to bring
And make the daylight still a happy thing,
And tender voices, to make soft the wind:
But if it were not so – if I could find
No love in all this world for comforting,
Nor any path but hollowly did ring
Where "dust to dust" the love from life disjoin'd;
And if, before those sepulchres unmoving
I stood alone (as some forsaken lamb
Goes bleating up the moors in weary dearth)
Crying "Where are ye, O my loved and loving?" –
I know a voice would sound, "Daughter, I AM.
Can I suffice for Heaven and not for earth?"

Substitution

When some beloved voice that was to you
Both sound and sweetness, faileth suddenly,
And silence, against which you dare not cry,
Aches round you like a strong disease and new
What hope? what help? what music will undo
That silence to your sense? Not friendship's sigh,
Not reason's subtle count; not melody
Of viols, nor of pipes that Faunus blew;
Not songs of poets, nor of nightingales
Whose hearts leap upward through the cypress-trees
To the clear moon; nor yet the spheric laws
Self-chanted, nor the angels' sweet "All hails,"
Met in the smile of God: nay, none of these.
Speak thou, availing Christ! and fill this pause.

An Apprehension

If all the gentlest-hearted friends I know
Concentred in one heart their gentleness,
That still grew gentler till its pulse was less
For life than pity, I should yet be slow
To bring my own heart nakedly below
The palm of such a friend, that he should press
Motive, condition, means, appliances,

My false ideal joy and fickle woe,
Out full to light and knowledge; I should fear
Some plait between the brows, some rougher chime
In the free voice. O angels, let your flood
Of bitter scorn dash on me! do ye hear
What I say who hear calmly all the time
This everlasting face to face with God?

The Soul's Expression

With stammering lips and insufficient sound
I strive and struggle to deliver right
That music of my nature, day and night
With dream and thought and feeling interwound
And inly answering all the senses round
With octaves of a mystic depth and height
Which step out grandly to the infinite
From the dark edges of the sensual ground.
This song of soul I struggle to outbear
Through portals of the sense, sublime and whole,
And utter all myself into the air:
But if I did it, as the thunder-roll
Breaks its own cloud, my flesh would perish there,
Before that dread apocalypse of soul.

To Flush, My Dog *(Extract)*

***

Blessings on thee, dog of mine,
Pretty collars make thee fine,
Sugared milk make fat thee!
Pleasures wag on in thy tail –
Hands of gentle motion fail
Nevermore, to pat thee!

Downy pillow take thy head,
Silken coverlid bestead,
Sunshine help thy sleeping!
No fly's buzzing wake thee up –
No man break thy purple cup,
Set for drinking deep in.

Whiskered cats arointed flee –
Sturdy stoppers keep from thee
Cologne distillations;
Nuts lie in thy path for stones,
And thy feast – day macaroons
Turn to daily rations!

Mock I thee, in wishing weal? –
Tears are in my eyes to feel
Thou art made so straightly,
Blessing needs must straighten too, –
Little canst thou joy or do,
Thou who lovest greatly.

Yet be blessed to the height
Of all good and all delight
Pervious to thy nature, –
Only loved beyond that line,
With a love that answers thine,
Loving fellow – creature!

The Pet-Name *(Extract)*

***

My brother gave that name to me
When we were children twain,
When names acquired baptismally
Were hard to utter, as to see
That life had any pain.

No shade was on us then, save one
Of chestnuts from the hill
And through the word our laugh did run
As part thereof.
The mirth being done,
He calls me bv it still.

Nay, do not smile! I hear in it
What none of you can hear,
The talk upon the willow seat,
The bird and wind that did repeat
Around, our human cheer.

I hear the birthday's noisy bliss,
My sisters' woodland glee,
My father's praise, I did not miss,
When stooping down he cared to kiss
The poet at his knee, –

And voices, which, to name me, aye
Their tenderest tones were keeping
To some I never more can say
An answer, till God wipes away
In heaven these drops of weeping.

My name to me a sadness wears,
No murmurs cross my mind.
Now God be thanked for these thick tears.
Which show, of those departed years.
Sweet memories left behind.

Now God be thanked for years enwrought
With love which softens yet:
Now God be thanked for every thought
Which is so tender it has caught
Earth's guerdon of regret.

Earth saddens, never shall remove
Affections purely given;
And e'en that mortal grief shall prove
The immortality of love,
And heighten it with Heaven.

***

Chapter Two: Death & Spirituality

Faith was a constant comfort for Barrett Browning and her spiritual poems fused religious themes with frustration over her own human reality.

Religion played a central part in Elizabeth's life – such was the expectation for women in Britain during the early 1800s. Though, unlike typical girls her age, EBB had such a ferocious appetite for knowledge that she taught herself enough Hebrew to read the Old Testament from start to finish by the time she was a teenager. She played an active part in the missionary societies of her local church, seeing it as an avenue for activism where politics was not so accepting of females.

Unlike her brothers, who had been sent away for formal education, Elizabeth was expected to stay at home to study. It was around this time that her access to the outside world became restricted by her health, and her spiritual connection with God intensified. Her exploration of religion ranges from the simplistic and idealistic, in 'A Child's Thoughts of God' to complex musings about the meaning of life in 'Human Life's Mystery': a subject that plagued her during illness and times of mourning.

Death became a common theme in her poetry with weeks on end spent in isolation. Beautiful imagery of Heaven and the angels suggests that she sought comfort in the idea of a divine world beyond her own. She even seemed accepting of her fate. Her poems portrayed death in a positive way and she was known to have seen her mother's passing – as well as that of poet William Cowper in 'Cowper's Grave' – as a release from suffering, rather than an act of evil.

Her shorter poems, such as 'Futurity' and 'Comfort', examine the minutia of everyday emotions and struggles, hinting that, for long periods of her life, she was frustrated with the shortcomings of the human condition but enthusiastic about some higher order.

A Child's Thought of God

They say that God lives very high;
But if you look above the pines
You cannot see our God; and why?

And if you dig down in the mines,
You never see Him in the gold,
Though from Him all that's glory shines.

God is so good, He wears a fold
Of heaven and earth across His face,
Like secrets kept, for love, untold.

But still I feel that His embrace
Slides down by thrills, through all things made,
Through sight and sound of every place;

As if my tender mother laid
On my shut lids her kisses' pressure,
Half waking me at night, and said,
"Who kissed you through the dark, dear guesser?"

Human Life's Mystery (*Extract*)

We sow the glebe, we reap the corn,
We build the house where we may rest,
And then, at moments, suddenly,
We look up to the great wide sky,
Inquiring wherefore we were born...
For earnest or for jest?

***

God keeps His holy mysteries
Just on the outside of man's dream;
In diapason slow, we think
To hear their pinions rise and sink,
While they float pure beneath His eyes,
Like swans adown a stream.

Abstractions, are they, from the forms
Of His great beauty? – exaltations
From His great glory? – strong previsions
Of what we shall be? – intuitions
Of what we are, – in calms and storms,
Beyond our peace and passions?

From 'The Soul's Travelling'

God, God!
With a child's voice I cry,
Weak, sad, confidingly –
God, God!
Thou knowest, eyelids, raised not always up
Unto Thy love (as none of ours are), droop
As ours, o'er many a tear!
Thou knowest, though Thy universe is broad,
Two little tears suffice to cover all:
Thou knowest, Thou, who art so prodigal
Of beauty, we are oft but stricken deer
Expiring in the woods – that care for none
Of those delightsome flowers they die upon.

O blissful Mouth which breathed the mournful breath
We name our souls, self-spoilt! – by that strong passion
Which paled Thee once with sighs, – by that strong death
Which made Thee once unbreathing – from the wrack
Themselves have called around them, call them back,
Back to Thee in continuous aspiration!
For here, O Lord,
For here they travel vainly, – vainly pass
From city-pavement to untrodden sward,
Where the lark finds her deep nest in the grass
Cold with the earth's last dew. Yea, very vain
The greatest speed of all these souls of men
Unless they travel upward to the throne

Where sittest THOU, the satisfying ONE,
With help for sins and holy perfectings
For all requirements – while the archangel, raising
Unto Thy face his full ecstatic gazing,
Forgets the rush and rapture of his wings.

Sabbath Morning at Sea (*Extract*)

***

Love me, sweet friends, this sabbath day.
The sea sings round me while ye roll
Afar the hymn, unaltered,
And kneel, where once I knelt to pray,
And bless me deeper in your soul
Because your voice has faltered.

And though this sabbath comes to me
Without the stolèd minister,
And chanting congregation,
God's Spirit shall give comfort.
He who brooded soft on waters drear,
Creator on creation.

He shall assist me to look higher,
Where keep the saints, with harp and song,
An endless sabbath morning,
And, on that sea commixed with fire.
Oft drop their eyelids raised too long
To the full Godhead's burning.

A Seaside Walk

We walked beside the sea,
After a day which perished silently
Of its own glory, like the Princess weird
Who, combating the Genius, scorched and seared,
Uttered with burning breath, "Ho! victory!"
And sank adown, an heap of ashes pale;
So runs the Arab tale.

The sky above us showed
An universal and unmoving cloud,
On which, the cliffs permitted us to see
Only the outline of their majesty,
As master-minds, when gazed at by the crowd!
And, shining with a gloom, the water grey
Swang in its moon-taught way.

Nor moon nor stars were out.
They did not dare to tread so soon about,
Though trembling, in the footsteps of the sun.
The light was neither night's nor day's, but one
Which, life-like, had a beauty in its doubt;
And Silence's impassioned breathings round
Seemed wandering into sound.

O solemn-beating heart
Of nature! I have knowledge that thou art
Bound unto man's by cords he cannot sever,
And, what time they are slackened by him ever,

So to attest his own supernal part,
Still runneth thy vibration fast and strong,
The slackened cord along.

For though we never spoke
Of the grey water anal the shaded rock,
Dark wave and stone, unconsciously, were fused
Into the plaintive speaking that we used,
Of absent friends and memories unforsook;
And, had we seen each other's face, we had
Seen haply, each was sad.

Work

What are we set on earth for? Say, to toil;
Nor seek to leave thy tending of the vines
For all the heat o' the day, till it declines,
And Death's mild curfew shall from work assoil.
God did anoint thee with his odorous oil,
To wrestle, not to reign; and He assigns
All thy tears over, like pure crystallines,
For younger fellow-workers of the soil
To wear for amulets. So others shall
Take patience, labor, to their heart and hand
From thy hand and thy heart and thy brave cheer,
And God's grace fructify through thee to
The least flower with a brimming cup may stand,
And share its dew-drop with another near.

The Deserted Garden *(Extract)*

***

My childhood from my life is parted,
My footstep from the moss which drew
Its fairy circle round: anew
The garden is deserted.

Another thrush may there rehearse
The madrigals which sweetest are;
No more for me! myself afar
Do sing a sadder verse.

Ah me, ah me! when erst I lay
In that child's-nest so greenly wrought,
I laughed unto myself and thought
"The time will pass away."

And still I laughed, and did not fear
But that, whene'er was past away
The childish time, some happier play
My womanhood would cheer.
I knew the time would pass away,
And yet, beside the rose-tree wall,
Dear God, how seldom, if at all,
Did I look up to pray!

The time is past; and now that grows
The cypress high among the trees,
And I behold white sepulchres
As well as the white rose,

When graver, meeker thoughts are given,
And I have learnt to lift my face,
Reminded how earth's greenest place
The colour draws from heaven,

It something saith for earthly pain,
But more for Heavenly promise free,
That I who was, would shrink to be
That happy child again.

Aurora Leigh: Book VIII (*Extract*)

***

"Could we sit
Just so for ever, sweetest friend," he said,
"My failure would seem better than success.
And yet indeed your book has dealt with me
More gently, cousin, than you ever will!
Your book brought down entire the bright June-day,
And set me wandering in the garden-walks,
And let me watch the garland in a place
You blushed so ... nay, forgive me, do not stir, –
I only thank the book for what it taught,
And what permitted. Poet, doubt yourself,
But never doubt that you're a poet to me
From henceforth. You have written poems, sweet,
Which moved me in secret, as the sap is moved
In still March-branches, signless as a stone:
But this last book o'ercame me like soft rain
Which falls at midnight, when the tightened bark
Breaks out into unhesitating buds
And sudden protestations of the spring.
In all your other books, I saw but you:
A man may see the moon so, in a pond,
And not be nearer therefore to the moon,
Nor use the sight ... except to drown himself:
And so I forced my heart back from the sight,

For what had I, I thought, to do with her,
Aurora ... Romney? But, in this last book,
You showed me something separate from yourself,
Beyond you, and I bore to take it in
And let it draw me. You have shown me truths,
O June-day friend, that help me now at night,
When June is over! truths not yours, indeed,
But set within my reach by means of you,
Presented by your voice and verse the way
To take them clearest. Verily I was wrong;
And verily many thinkers of this age,
Ay, many Christian teachers, half in heaven,
Are wrong in just my sense who understood
Our natural world too insularly, as if
No spiritual counterpart completed it,
Consummating its meaning, rounding all
To justice and perfection, line by line,
Form by form, nothing single nor alone,
The great below clenched by the great above,
Shade here authenticating substance there,
The body proving spirit, as the effect
The cause: we meantime being too grossly apt
To hold the natural, as dogs a bone
(Though reason and nature beat us in the face),
So obstinately, that we'll break our teeth
Or ever we let go. For everywhere
We're too materialistic, – eating clay
(Like men of the west) instead of Adam's corn

And Noah's wine – clay by handfuls, clay by lumps,
Until we're filled up to the throat with clay,
And grow the grimy colour of the ground
On which we are feeding. Ay, materialist
The age's name is. God Himself, with some,
Is apprehended as the bare result
Of what His hand materially has made,
Expressed in such an algebraic sign
Called God – that is, to put it otherwise,
They add up nature to a nought of God
And cross the quotient. There are many even,
Whose names are written in the Christian Church
To no dishonour, diet still on mud
And splash the altars with it. You might think
The clay, Christ laid upon their eyelids when,
Still blind, he called them to the use of sight,
Remained there to retard its exercise
With clogging incrustations. Close to heaven,
They see, for mysteries, through the open doors,
Vague puffs of smoke from pots of earthenware;
And fain would enter, when their time shall come,
With quite a different body than St. Paul
Has promised, – husk and chaff, the whole barley-corn,
Or where's the resurrection?'

***

✹✹✹ Critique: 'Aurora Leigh: Book VIII'

To understand this poem fully we must trace the lineage of its narrators: Barrett Browning is writing about a woman poet, Aurora Leigh, writing about writing as the woman poet, Aurora Leigh. She employs the blank verse form to build the narrative over a nine-book structure, its conversational tone extending and elucidating the evolution of Aurora, and by association Barrett Browning's themes, ideas and the relationships therein.

Here, in this extract of lines 581–645, the poet reveals to us the extraordinary effect that Aurora's poem has had on Aurora's lover, the initially sceptical Romney: "But this last book o'ercame me like soft rain / Which falls at midnight, when the tightened bark / Breaks out into unhesitating buds / And sudden protestations of the spring."

We are being shown, as is Aurora, how the reading of her poem is developing the internal character of her friend and love interest. It is not a high-minded spiritualism she seeks for her readers but an everyday one; Romney speaks of the rain and the seasons "the great below clenched by the great above".

What we are privy to are the moments of the poem's creation and its effect rather than its content; we are viewing behind the scenes as if invited on to a film set to watch a movie being made that we never see. We can only read Romney's reactions to the poem, not the poem he has felt so deeply. The reader comes away asking the same questions as the poets: what is it to be a complete artist and therefore by extension a complete person?

In this beautiful passage, both the male and female souls have been stretched and fulfilled by the same poem; the woman in the writing and the man in the reading. And the answer to these questions is enacted through the nature of the individual's relationship to the spiritual and to God: by being a poet she has been able to draw a spiritual realm in the material everyday world of ordinary people. Aurora's desire for a "new world all alive with creatures, new sun, new moon, new flowers, new people" (Book VII, lines 1199–1200) is almost fulfilled in this passage and Romney capitulates, finally understanding what the poet's vision will engender.

A Thought for a Lonely Death-Bed

If God compel thee to this destiny,
To die alone, with none beside thy bed
To ruffle round with sobs thy last word said
And mark with tears the pulses ebb from thee,
Pray then alone, 'O Christ, come tenderly!
By thy forsaken Sonship in the red
Drear wine-press, by the wilderness out-spread,
And the lone garden where thine agony
Fell bloody from thy brow, – by all of those
Permitted desolations, comfort mine!
No earthly friend being near me, interpose
No deathly angel 'twixt my face aud thine,
But stoop Thyself to gather my life's rose,
And smile away my mortal to Divine!'

The Sleep (*Extract*)

***

Aye, men may wonder while they scan
A living, thinking, feeling man
Confirmed in such a rest to keep;
But angels say, and through the word
I think their happy smile is heard–
"He giveth His belovèd, sleep."

For me, my heart that erst did go
Most like a tired child at a show,
That sees through tears the mummers leap,
Would now its wearied vision close,
Would child-like on His love repose,
Who giveth His belovèd, sleep.

And, friends, dear friends,– when it shall be
That this low breath is gone from me,
And round my bier ye come to weep,
Let One, most loving of you all,
Say, "Not a tear must o'er her fall;
He giveth His belovèd, sleep."

Cowper's Grave (*Extract*)

***

He shall be strong to sanctify the poet's high vocation,
And bow the meekest Christian down in meeker adoration;
Nor ever shall he be, in praise, by wise or good forsaken.
Named sottly as the household name of one whom God hath taken.

With quiet sadness and no gloom I learn to think upon him.
With meekness that is gratefulness to God whose heaven hath
won him, –
Who suffered once the madness-cloud to his own love to blind him.
But gently led the blind along where breath and bird could find him;

And wrought within his shattered brain such quick poetic senses
As hills have language for, and stars harmonious influences!
The pulse of dew upon the grass kept his within its number.
And silent shadow from the trees refreshed him like a slumber.

Died (*Extract*)

***

Dead. Man's "I was" by God's "I am" –
All hero-worship comes to that.
High heart, high thought, high fame, as flat
As a gravestone. Bring your Jacet jam--
The epitaph's an epigram.

Dead. There's an answer to arrest
All carping. Dust's his natural place?
He'll let the flies buzz round his face
And, though you slander, not protest?
From such an one, exact the Best?

Opinions gold or brass are null.
We chuck our flattery or abuse,
Called Caesar's due, as Charon's dues,
I' the teeth of some dead sage or fool,
To mend the grinning of a skull.

Be abstinent in praise and blame.
The man's still mortal, who stands first,
And mortal only, if last and worst.
Then slowly lift so frail a fame,
Or softly drop so poor a shame.

The Autumn

Go, sit upon the lofty hill,
And turn your eyes around,
Where waving woods and waters wild
Do hymn an autumn sound.
The summer sun is faint on them –
The summer flowers depart –
Sit still – as all transform'd to stone,
Except your musing heart.

How there you sat in summer-time,
May yet be in your mind;
And how you heard the green woods sing
Beneath the freshening wind.
Though the same wind now blows around,
You would its blast recall;
For every breath that stirs the trees,
Doth cause a leaf to fall.

Oh! like that wind, is all the mirth
That flesh and dust impart:
We cannot bear its visitings,
When change is on the heart.
Gay words and jests may make us smile,
When Sorrow is asleep;
But other things must make us smile,
When Sorrow bids us weep!

The dearest hands that clasp our hands, –
Their presence may be o'er;
The dearest voice that meets our ear,
That tone may come no more!
Youth fades; and then, the joys of youth,
Which once refresh'd our mind,
Shall come – as, on those sighing woods,
The chilling autumn wind.

Hear not the wind – view not the woods;
Look out o'er vale and hill –
In spring, the sky encircled them –
The sky is round them still.
Come autumn's scathe – come winter's cold –
Come change – and human fate!
Whatever prospect Heaven doth bound,
Can ne'er be desolate.

Earth (*Extract*)

How beautiful is earth! my starry thoughts
Look down on it from their unearthly sphere,
And sing symphonious – Beautiful is earth!
The lights and shadows of her myriad hills;
The branching greenness of her myriad woods;
Her sky-affecting rocks; her zoning sea;
Her rushing, gleaming cataracts; her streams
That race below, the wingëd clouds on high;
Her pleasantness of vale and meadow! –

***

Patience Taught by Nature

"O dreary life," we cry, "O dreary life!"
And still the generations of the birds
Sing through our sighing, and the flocks and herds
Serenely live while we are keeping strife
With Heaven's true purpose in us, as a knife
Against which we may struggle! Ocean girds
Unslackened the dry land: savannah-swards
Unweary sweep: hills watch unworn, and rife
Meek leaves drop yearly from the forest-trees
To show, above, the unwasted stars that pass
In their old glory. O thou God of old!
Grant me some smaller grace than comes to *these*: –
But so much patience, as a blade of grass
Grows by, contented through the heat and cold.

Cheerfulness Taught by Reason

I think we are too ready with complaint
In this fair world of God's. Had we no hope
Indeed beyond the zenith and the slope
Of yon gray blank of sky, we might grow faint
To muse upon eternity's constraint
Round our aspirant souls; but since the scope
Must widen early, is it well to droop,
For a few days consumed in loss and taint?
O pusillanimous Heart, be comforted
And, like a cheerful traveller, take the road
Singing beside the hedge. What if the bread
Be bitter in thine inn, and thou unshod
To meet the flints? At least it may be said
"Because the way is short, I thank thee, God."

De Profundis

The face, which, duly as the sun,
Rose up for me with life begun,
To mark all bright hours of the day
With hourly love, is dimmed away –
And yet my days go on, go on.

The tongue which, like a stream, could run
Smooth music from the roughest stone,
And every morning with "Good day"
Make each day good, is hushed away,
And yet my days go on, go on.

The heart which, like a staff, was one
For mine to lean and rest upon,
The strongest on the longest day
With steadfast love, is caught away,
And yet my days go on, go on.

And cold before my summer's done,
And deaf in Nature's general tune,
And fallen too low for special fear,
And here, with hope no longer here,
While the tears drop, my days go on.

The world goes whispering to its own,
"This anguish pierces to the bone; "
And tender friends go sighing round,
"What love can ever cure this wound?"
My days go on, my days go on.

The past rolls forward on the sun
And makes all night. O dreams begun,
Not to be ended! Ended bliss,
And life that will not end in this!
My days go on, my days go on.

Breath freezes on my lips to moan:
As one alone, once not alone,
I sit and knock at Nature's door,
Heart-bare, heart-hungry, very poor,
Whose desolated days go on.

I knock and cry, – Undone, undone!
Is there no help, no comfort, – none?
No gleaning in the wide wheat plains
Where others drive their loaded wains?
My vacant days go on, go on.

***

He reigns above, He reigns alone;
Systems burn out and have his throne;
Fair mists of seraphs melt and fall
Around Him, changeless amid all,
Ancient of Days, whose days go on.

He reigns below, He reigns alone,
And, having life in love forgone
Beneath the crown of sovran thorns,
He reigns the Jealous God. Who mourns
Or rules with Him, while days go on?

By anguish which made pale the sun,
I hear Him charge his saints that none
Among his creatures anywhere
Blaspheme against Him with despair,
However darkly days go on.

Take from my head the thorn-wreath brown!
No mortal grief deserves that crown.
O supreme Love, chief misery,
The sharp regalia are for Thee
Whose days eternally go on!

For us, – whatever's undergone,
Thou knowest, willest what is done,
Grief may be joy misunderstood;
Only the Good discerns the good.
I trust Thee while my days go on.

Whatever's lost, it first was won;
We will not struggle nor impugn.
Perhaps the cup was broken here,
That Heaven's new wine might show more clear.
I praise Thee while my days go on.

I praise Thee while my days go on;
I love Thee while my days go on:
Through dark and dearth, through fire and frost,
With emptied arms and treasure lost,
I thank Thee while my days go on.

And having in thy life-depth thrown
Being and suffering (which are one),
As a child drops his pebble small
Down some deep well, and hears it fall
Smiling – so I. THY DAYS GO ON.

✸✸✸ Critique: *'De Profundis'*

The title is the opening line of Psalm 130, often used in the liturgy of the dead: *de profundis clamavi ad te, Domine*, "from the depths I cried out to thee, Lord." The same words were the title of a letter written by Oscar Wilde to express his own despair at his imprisonment.

This is Barrett Browning's plea for divine mercy from a well of deep despair. It was written after the double loss of her brothers within six months of each other – the first, Samuel, of yellow fever in Jamacia and the second, her favourite brother "Bro", drowned off the coast of Torquay, two miles from where she had come to rehabilitate her health from the benefits of its sea air. EBB uses the poem as both a lament and a therapeutic tool; she is willing the light to break through the dark days and return her to equilibrium and a trust in God. The juxtaposition of mundane greetings like "good day" with the weight of her sorrow "I knock and cry, – Undone, undone!" emphasize the dissonance between her inner turmoil and the external world which has become flat and hollow.

Barrett Browning's journey through her grief is further complicated by her feelings of guilt surrounding her brothers' deaths. She grapples with questions of divine justice, asking rhetorically, "He reigns with a Jealous God. Who mourns / Or rules with Him, while days go on?"

Having increasingly become interested in the sonnet form after these deaths, she wrote the 'Grief', alluding to the fact that it is those who are silent who suffer it most keenly – the form allowing her to contain and release her emotions. But this poem's rhythm and pace is treading water through an ocean of grief. The words "And yet my days go on my days go on" display the weight and noise of her sorrow while giving space for redemption. As the poem progresses, Elizabeth transitions from her personal grief toward a broader spiritual perspective. The biblical imagery, the "crown of sovereign thorns," recalls the Passion.

Ultimately, 'De Profundis' is a testament to Barrett Browning's emotional depth and resilience. While she mourns her brother "Bro" and grapples with her physical ailments, she also expresses a burgeoning faith that sustains her. The lines in stanza XXIII encapsulate this duality: "I praise Thee while my days go on; / I love Thee while my days go on."

Through this work, EBB lays the groundwork for her later works, such as *Aurora Leigh*, as poem "outlets" for themes of spirituality and personal struggle. This poem marks a significant moment in her artistic journey, showcasing her ability to transform personal grief into narratives that speak to universal human experiences, not only netting her own pain but also inviting readers to reflect on their own struggles and the resilience of the human spirit.

A Dead Rose

O Rose! who dares to name thee?
No longer roseate now, nor soft, nor sweet;
But pale, and hard, and dry, as stubble-wheat, –
Kept seven years in a drawer – thy titles shame thee.

The breeze that used to blow thee
Between the hedgerow thorns, and take away
An odour up the lane to last all day, –
If breathing now, – unsweetened would forego thee.

The sun that used to smite thee,
And mix his glory in thy gorgeous urn,
Till beam appeared to bloom, and flower to burn, –
If shining now, – with not a hue would light thee.

The dew that used to wet thee,
And, white first, grow incarnadined, because
It lay upon thee where the crimson was, –
If dropping now, – would darken where it met thee.

The fly that lit upon thee,
To stretch the tendrils of its tiny feet,
Along thy leaf's pure edges, after heat, –
If lighting now, – would coldly overrun thee.

The bee that once did suck thee,
And build thy perfumed ambers up his hive,
And swoon in thee for joy, till scarce alive, –
If passing now, – would blindly overlook thee.

The heart doth recognise thee,
Alone, alone! The heart doth smell thee sweet,
Doth view thee fair, doth judge thee most complete, –
Though seeing now those changes that disguise thee.

Yes, and the heart doth owe thee
More love, dead rose! than to such roses bold
As Julia wears at dances, smiling cold! –
Lie still upon this heart – which breaks below thee!

Insufficiency

When I attain to utter forth in verse
Some inward thought, my soul throbs audibly
Along my pulses, yearning to be free
And something farther, fuller, higher, rehearse
To the individual, true, and the universe,
In consummation of right harmony:
But, like a wind-exposed distorted tree,
We are blown against for ever by the curse
Which breathes through Nature. Oh, the world is weak!
The effluence of each is false to all,
And what we best conceive we fail to speak.
Wait, soul, until thine ashen garments fall,
And then resume thy broken strains, and seek
Fit peroration without let or thrall.

Adequacy

Now, by the verdure on thy thousand hills,
Beloved England, doth the earth appear
Quite good enough for men to overbear
The will of God in, with rebellious wills!
We cannot say the morning-sun fulfils
Ingloriously its course, nor that the clear
Strong stars without significance insphere
Our habitation: we, meantime, our ills
Heap up against this good and lift a cry
Against this work-day world, this ill-spread feast,
As if ourselves were better certainly
Than what we come to. Maker and High Priest,
I ask thee not my joys to multiply,
Only to make me worthier of the least.

Exaggeration

We overstate the ills of life, and take
Imagination (given us to bring down
The choirs of singing angels overshone
By God's clear glory) down our earth to rake
The dismal snows instead, flake following flake,
To cover all the corn; we walk upon
The shadow of hills across a level thrown,
And pant like climbers: near the alder brake
We sigh so loud, the nightingale within
Refuses to sing loud, as else she would.
O brothers, let us leave the shame and sin
Of taking vainly, in a plaintive mood,
The holy name of grief! holy herein
That by the grief of one came all our good.

Discontent

Light human nature is too lightly tost
And ruffled without cause, complaining on
Restless with rest, until, being overthrown,
It learneth to lie quiet. Let a frost
Or a small wasp have crept to the inner-most
Of our ripe peach, or let the wilful sun
Shine westward of our window, straight we run
A furlong's sigh as if the world were lost.
But what time through the heart and through the brain
God hath transfixed us, we, so moved before,
Attain to a calm. Ay, shouldering weights of pain,
We anchor in deep waters, safe from shore,
And hear submissive o'er the stormy main
God's chartered judgments walk for evermore.

Comfort

Speak low to me, my Saviour, low and sweet
From out the hallelujahs, sweet and low
Lest I should fear and fall, and miss Thee so
Who art not missed by any that entreat.
Speak to mo as to Mary at thy feet!
And if no precious gums my hands bestow,
Let my tears drop like amber while I go
In reach of thy divinest voice complete
In humanest affection, thus, in sooth,
To lose the sense of losing. As a child,
Whose song-bird seeks the wood for evermore
Is sung to in its stead by mother's mouth
Till, sinking on her breast, love-reconciled,
He sleeps the faster that he wept before.

Irreparableness

I have been in the meadows all the day
And gathered there the nosegay that you see
Singing within myself as bird or bee
When such do field-work on a morn of May.
But, now I look upon my flowers, decay
Has met them in my hands more fatally
Because more warmly clasped, – and sobs are free
To come instead of songs. What do you say,
Sweet counsellors, dear friends? that I should go
Back straightway to the fields and gather more?
Another, sooth, may do it, but not I!
My heart is very tired, my strength is low,
My hands are full of blossoms plucked before,
Held dead within them till myself shall die.

A Musical Instrument

What was he doing, the great god Pan,
Down in the reeds by the river?
Spreading ruin and scattering ban,
Splashing and paddling with hoofs of a goat,
And breaking the golden lilies afloat
With the dragon-fly on the river.

He tore out a reed, the great god Pan,
From the deep cool bed of the river:
The limpid water turbidly ran,
And the broken lilies a-dying lay,
And the dragon-fly had fled away,
Ere he brought it out of the river.

High on the shore sate the great god Pan,
While turbidly flowed the river;
And hacked and hewed as a great god can,
With his hard bleak steel at the patient reed,
Till there was not a sign of a leaf indeed
To prove it fresh from the river.

He cut it short, did the great god Pan,
(How tall it stood in the river!)
Then drew the pith, like the heart of a man,
Steadily from the outside ring,
And notched the poor dry empty thing
In holes, as he sate by the river.

"This is the way," laughed the great god Pan,
(Laughed while he sat by the river)
"The only way, since gods began
To make sweet music, they could succeed."
Then, dropping his mouth to a hole in the reed,
He blew in power by the river.

Sweet, sweet, sweet, O Pan!
Piercing sweet by the river!
Blinding sweet, O great god Pan!
The sun on the hill forgot to die,
And the lilies revived, and the dragon-fly
Came back to dream on the river.

Yet half a beast is the great god Pan,
To laugh as he sits by the river,
Making a poet out of a man:
The true gods sigh for the cost and pain,
For the reed which grows nevermore again
As a reed with the reeds in the river.

Perplexed Music

Experience, like a pale musician, holds
A dulcimer of patience in his hand,
Whence harmonies, we cannot understand,
Of God; will in his worlds, the strain unfolds
In sad-perplexed minors: deathly colds
Fall on us while we hear, and countermand
Our sanguine heart back from the fancyland
With nightingales in visionary wolds.
We murmur "Where is any certain tune
Or measured music in such notes as these?"
But angels, leaning from the golden seat,
Are not so minded their fine ear hath won
The issue of completed cadences,
And, smiling down the stars, they whisper –
SWEET.

Futurity

And, O beloved voices, upon which
Ours passionately call because erelong
Ye brake off in the middle of that song
We sang together softly, to enrich
The poor world with the sense of love, and witch,
The heart out of things evil, I am strong,
Knowing ye are not lost for aye among

The hills, with last year's thrush. God keeps a niche
In Heaven to hold our idols; and albeit
He brake them to our faces and denied
That our close kisses should impair their white,
I know we shall behold them raised, complete,
The dust swept from their beauty, glorified
New Memnons singing in the great God-light.

The Weakest Thing

Which is the weakest thing of all
Mine heart can ponder?
The sun, a little cloud can pall
With darkness yonder?
The cloud, a little wind can move
Where'er it listeth?
The wind, a little leaf above,
Though sere, resisteth?

What time that yellow leaf was green,
My days were gladder;
But now, whatever Spring may mean,
I must grow sadder.
Ah me! a leaf with sighs can wring
My lips asunder
Then is mine heart the weakest thing
Itself can ponder.

Yet, Heart, when sun and cloud are pined
And drop together,
And at a blast, which is not wind,
The forests wither,
Thou, from the darkening deathly curse
To glory breakest,
The Strongest of the universe
Guarding the weakest!

Past and Future

My future will not copy fair my past
On any leaf but Heaven's. Be fully done,
Supernal Will! I would not fain be one
Who, satisfying thirst and breaking fast
Upon the fulness of the heart, at last
Saith no grace after meat. My wine hath run
Indeed out of my cup, and there is none
To gather up the bread of my repast
Scattered and trampled! Yet I find some good
In earth's green herbs, and streams that bubble up
Clear from the darkling ground, content until
I sit with angels before better food.
Dear Christ! when thy new vintage fills my cup,
This hand shall shake no more, nor that wine spill.

Chorus of Eden Spirits

Hearken, oh hearken! let your souls behind you
Turn, gently moved!
Our voices feel along the Dread to find you,
O lost, beloved!
Through the thick-shielded and strong-marshalled
angels,
They press and pierce:
Our requiems follow fast on our evangels,
Voice throbs in verse.
We are but orphaned spirits left in Eden
A time ago:
God gave us golden cups, and we were bidden
To feed you so.
But now our right hand hath no cup remaining,
No work to do,
The mystic hydromel is spilt, and staining
The whole earth through.
Most ineradicable stains, for showing
(Not interfused!)
That brighter colours were the world's foregoing,
Than shall be used.
Hearken, oh hearken! ye shall hearken surely
For years and years,
The noise beside you, dripping coldly, purely,
Of spirits' tears.

The yearning to a beautiful denied you,
Shall strain your powers.
Ideal sweetnesses shall over-glide you,
Resumed from ours.
In all your music, our pathetic minor
Your ears shall cross;
And all good gifts shall mind you of diviner,
With sense of loss.
We shall be near you in your poet-languors
And wild extremes,
What time ye vex the desert with vain angers,
Or mock with dreams.
And when upon you, weary after roaming,
Death's seal is put,
By the foregone ye shall discern the coming,
Through eyelids shut.

The Look

The Saviour looked on Peter. Ay, no word,
No gesture of reproach; the Heavens serene
Though heavy with armed justice, did not lean
Their thunders that way: the forsaken Lord
Looked only, on the traitor. None record
What that look was, none guess; for those who have seen
Wronged lovers loving through a death-pang keen,
Or pale-cheeked martyrs smiling to a sword,
Have missed Jehovah at the judgment-call.
And Peter, from the height of blasphemy
"I never knew this man" did quail and fall
As knowing straight that God; and turned free
And went out speechless from the face of all
And filled the silence, weeping bitterly.

The Two Sayings

Two savings of the Holy Scriptures beat
Like pulses in the Church's brow and breast;
And by them we find rest in our unrest
And, heart deep in salt-tears, do yet entreat
God's fellowship as if on heavenly seat.
The first is Jesus wept, whereon is prest

Full many a sobbing face that drops its best
And sweetest waters on the record sweet:
And one is where the Christ, denied and scorned
Looked upon Peter. Oh, to render plain
By help of having loved a little and mourned,
That look of sovran love and sovran pain
Which He, who could not sin yet suffered, turned
On him who could reject but not sustain!

Tears

Thank God, bless God, all ye who suffer not
More grief than ye can weep for. That is well
That is light grieving! lighter, none befell
Since Adam forfeited the primal lot.
Tears! what are tears? The babe weeps in its cot,
The mother singing, at her marriage-bell
The bride weeps, and before the oracle
Of high-faned hills the poet has forgot
Such moisture on his cheeks. Thank God for grace,
Ye who weep only! If, as some have done,
Ye grope tear-blinded in a desert place
And touch but tombs, look up I those tears will run
Soon in long rivers down the lifted face,
And leave the vision clear for stars and sun.

The Seraphim *(Extract)*

***

Zerah. A woman kneels
The mid cross under,
With white lips asunder,
And motion on each.
They throb, as she feels,
With a spasm, not a speech;
And her lids, close as sleep,
Are less calm, for the eyes
Have made room there to weep
Drop on drop –

Ador. Weep? Weep blood,
All women, all men!
He sweated it, He,
For your pale womanhood
And base manhood. Agree
That these water-tears, then,
Are vain, mocking like laughter:
Weep blood! Shall the flood
Of salt curses, whose foam is the darkness, on roll
Forward, on from the strand of the storm-beaten years,
And back from the rocks of the horrid hereafter,
And up, in a coil, from the present's wrath-spring,
Yea, down from the windows of heaven opening,
Deep calling to deep as they meet on his soul –
And men weep only tears?

***

Confessions (*Extract*)

***

Face to face in my chamber, my silent chamber, I saw her:
God and she and I only, there I sat down to draw her
Soul through the clefts of confession:
"Speak, I am holding thee fast,
As the angel of resurrection shall do at the last!"
"My cup is blood-red
With my sin," she said,
"And I pour it out to the bitter lees,
As if the angels of judgment stood over me strong at the last,
Or as thou wert as these."

A Child Asleep (*Extract*)

***

As the moths around a taper,
As the bees around a rose,
As the gnats around a vapour, –
So the Spirits group and close
Round about a holy childhood, as if drinking
its repose.:
Shapes of brightness overlean thee, –
Flash their diadems of youth
On the ringlets which half screen thee, –
While thou smilest, ... not in sooth
Thy smile ... but the overfair one, dropt from
some aethereal mouth.

Haply it is angels' duty,
During slumber, shade by shade:
To fine down this childish beauty
To the thing it must be made,
Ere the world shall bring it praises, or the tomb
shall see it fade.

Softly, softly! make no noises!
Now he lieth dead and dumb –
Now he hears the angels' voices
Folding silence in the room –
Now he muses deep the meaning of the
Heaven-words as they come.

Speak not! he is consecrated –
Breathe no breath across his eyes.
Lifted up and separated,
On the hand of God he lies,
In a sweetness beyond touching – held in
cloistral sanctities.

Could ye bless him – father –mother?
Bless the dimple in his cheek?
Dare ye look at one another,
And the benediction speak?
Would ye not break out in weeping, and
confess yourselves too weak?

He is harmless – ye are sinful, –
Ye are troubled – he, at ease:
From his slumber, virtue winful
Floweth outward with increase –
Dare not bless him! but be blessed by his peace –
and go in peace.

Chapter Three: Social Justice

These poems highlight Elizabeth's commitment to great causes, addressing child labour, slavery and women's rights, as well as fighting at home and overseas.

Secluded in her own home from the age of fifteen, the ailing Elizabeth spent an extraordinary amount of time reading about the world outside her windows. She developed a strong opposition to issues like slavery, child labour and wealth disparity. Yet for all her knowledge and opinions, as a woman in Victorian England she had no rights to vote, sue or fight in wars.

Instead, Elizabeth was a freedom fighter who used poetry as a platform for political dissent. "Freedom itself is a virtue, as well as a privilege," she wrote in the 1860 Preface to her political commentary *Poems before Congress*. She would not "excuse herself," she insisted, for views found to be unpopular or unpatriotic as she published the collection from her new home in Italy shortly after the outbreak of the Italian War of 1859.

Her poems took aim at the power men yielded over countries and their laws, in contrast to the helpless women left behind in war, mourning their fallen husbands and sons. In 'The Cry of the Children' and 'A Song for the Ragged Schools of London', she defends the working children of England – toiling in the mines and mills – in the hopes of bringing attention to their plight and changing the laws.

She was so fearless that she even condemned the views of her own family, creating a rift with her father that never healed. Her fervent anti-slavery campaigning conflicted with her upbringing, as a descendant of slaveholders who had acquired comfortable wealth from plantations in Jamaica. Her poem 'The Runaway Slave' was a career-defining piece of political poetry, taking controversial subject matter for its theme in a way that was shocking for a woman of her time.

The Prisoner

I count the dismal time by months and years
Since last I felt the green sward under foot,
And the great breath of all things summer –
Met mine upon my lips. Now earth appears
As strange to me as dreams of distant spheres
Or thoughts of Heaven we weep at. Nature's lute
Sounds on, behind this door so closely shut,
A strange wild music to the prisoner's ears,
Dilated by the distance, till the brain
Grows dim with fancies which it feels too
While ever, with a visionary pain,
Past the precluded senses, sweep and Rhine
Streams, forests, glades, and many a golden train
Of sunlit hills transfigured to Divine.

Hiram Powers' Greek Slave

They say Ideal beauty cannot enter
The house of anguish. On the threshold stands
An alien Image with enshackled hands,
Called the Greek Slave! as if the artist meant her
(That passionless perfection which he lent her,
Shadowed not darkened where the sill expands)
To so confront man's crimes in different lands
With man's ideal sense. Pierce to the centre,
Art's fiery finger! and break up ere long
The serfdom of this world. Appeal, fair stone,
From God's pure heights of beauty against man's
wrong! Catch up in thy divine face, not alone
East griefs but west, and strike and shame the strong,
By thunders of white silence, overthrown.

The Runaway Slave at Pilgrim's Point (*Extract*)

I STAND on the mark beside the shore
Of the first white pilgrim's bended knee,
Where exile turned to ancestor,
And God was thanked for liberty.
I have run through the night, my skin is as dark,
I bend my knee down on this mark...
I look on the sky and the sea.

O pilgrim-souls, I speak to you!
I see you come out proud and slow
From the land of the spirits pale as dew...
And round me and round me ye go!
O pilgrims, I have gasped and run
All night long from the whips of one
Who in your names works sin and woe.

And thus I thought that I would come
And kneel here where I knelt before,
And feel your souls around me hum
In undertone to the ocean's roar;
And lift my black face, my black hand,
Here, in your names, to curse this land
Ye blessed in freedom's evermore.

***

✹✹✹ Critique: 'The Runway Slave'

Written for the 1848 edition of *The Liberty Bell*, an abolitionist publication aimed at the women of Boston, the poem spans thirty-six verses and adopts the dramatic monologue form, which was emerging at the time as the "poetry of sympathy". Barrett Browning decided to employ this form to underscore her intention – to shock her audience.

Composed during her honeymoon while pregnant, the work showed her willingness to commit her literary talents to amplify the voices of the oppressed, even during what must have been a period of personal transformation. Perhaps she wanted to remedy the wrong that stemmed from her family's shameful past. She candidly expressed her feelings about this heritage in a letter to the artist, historian and critic John Ruskin, acknowledging the shame it brought her: "I belong to a family of West Indian slaveholders and if I believed in curses, I should be afraid."

In the long unfolding drama of the poem, the runaway describes being separated from the man she loved and raped by her master. The searing and direct tone is at once so clear and haunting, the urgent tones of the runaway audible, the tragic figure, physically close, is perhaps EBB's way of admitting to her part in history. The speaker explains to us why she has been driven to commit infanticide and will herself be murdered by the slave owners she is running from: "And the babe who lay on my bosom so, was far too white, too white for me" (line 115).

Browning's use of the repetition, narration, speech and syntax illustrates, to literary society, that poetry can be a tool for social justice. In her exposure of the voices of the oppressed, she is showing her support for female writers and their female subjects.

By inscribing the experiences of an unnamed fugitive slave woman within the geography of Pilgrim's Point, Browning ironically contrasts the narrative of liberty associated with the Mayflower. This ingenious inversion allows her to highlight the stark realities of slavery, as expressed through the slave woman's laments. A form of reportage that calls out to the "Pilgrim souls," blending plea with indictment. Its mastery is that it is, at times, hard to see where the poet ends and the speaker begins, where the pilgrim fathers end and the reader begins, its overarching message to this day inscribes its mark.

A Song for the Ragged Schools of London (*Extract*)

***

Lordly English, think it o'er,
Cæsar's doing is all undone!
You have cannons on your shore,
And free parliaments in London;

Princes' parks, and merchants' homes,
Tents for soldiers, ships for seamen, –
Ay, but ruins worse than Rome's,
In your pauper men and women.

Women leering through the gas
(Just such bosoms used to nurse you),
Men, turned wolves by famine – pass!
Those can speak themselves, and curse you.

But these others – children small,
Spilt like blots about the city,
Quay, and street, and palace-wall –
Take them up into your pity!

Ragged children with bare feet,
Whom the angels in white raiment,
Know the names of, to repeat
When they come on you for payment.

Ragged children with bare feet,
Huddled up out of the coldness
On your doorsteps, side by side,
Till your footman damns their boldness.

In the alleys, in the squares,
Begging, lying little rebels;
In the noisy thoroughfares,
Struggling on with piteous trebles.

The Cry of the Children (*Extract*)

***

"But, no!" say the children, weeping faster,
"He is speechless as a stone;
And they tell us, of His image is the master
Who commands us to work on.
Go to!" say the children, – "up in Heaven,
Dark, wheel–like, turning clouds are all we find!
Do not mock us; grief has made us unbelieving –
We look up for God, but tears have made us blind."
Do ye hear the children weeping and disproving,
O my brothers, what ye preach?
For God's possible is taught by His world's loving –
And the children doubt of each.

And well may the children weep before you;
They are weary ere they run;
They have never seen the sunshine, nor the glory
Which is brighter than the sun:
They know the grief of man, without its wisdom;
They sink in the despair, without its calm –
Are slaves, without the liberty in Christdom,–
Are martyrs, by the pang without the palm, –
Are worn, as if with age, yet unretrievingly
No dear remembrance keep, –
Are orphans of the earthly love and heavenly:
Let them weep! let them weep!

They look up, with their pale and sunken faces,
And their look is dread to see,
For they think you see their angels in their places,
With eyes meant for Deity; –
"How long," they say, "how long, O cruel nation,
Will you stand, to move the world, on a child's heart, –
Stifle down with a mailed heel its palpitation,
And tread onward to your throne amid the mart?
Our blood splashes upward, O our tyrants,
And your purple shews your path;
But the child's sob curseth deeper in the silence
Than the strong man in his wrath!"

A Curse for a Nation (*Extract*)

***

Because ye have broken your own chain
With the strain
Of brave men climbing a Nation's height,
Yet thence bear down with brand and thong
On souls of others, for this wrong
This is the curse. Write.

Because yourselves are standing straight
In the state
Of Freedom's foremost acolyte,
Yet keep calm footing all the time
On writhing bond – slaves, for this crime
This is the curse. Write.

Because ye prosper in God's name,
With a claim
To honor in the old world's sight,
Yet do the fiend's work perfectly
In strangling martyrs – for this lie
This is the curse. Write.

Ye shall watch while kings conspire
Round the people's smoldering fire,
And, warm for your part,
Shall never dare – O shame!
To utter the thought into flame
Which burns at your heart.
This is the curse. Write.

Ye shall watch while nations strive
With the bloodhounds, die or survive,
Drop faint from their jaws,
Or throttle them backward to death;
And only under your breath
Shall favor the cause.
This is the curse. Write.

Ye shall watch while strong men draw
The nets of feudal law
To strangle the weak;
And, counting the sin for a sin,
Your soul shall be sadder within
Than the word ye shall speak.
This is the curse. Write.

***

Casa Guidi Windows

I heard last night a little child go singing
'Neath Casa Guidi windows, by the church,
O bella liberta, O bella! – stringing
The same words still on notes he went in search
So high for, you concluded the upspringing
Of such a nimble bird to sky from perch
Must leave the whole bush in a tremble green,
And that the heart of Italy must beat,
While such a voice had leave to rise serene
'Twixt church and palace of a Florence street!
A little child, too, who not long had been
By mother's finger steadied on his feet,
And still *O bella liberta* he sang.

***

I wrote a meditation and a dream,
Hearing a little child sing in the street:
I leant upon his music as a theme,
Till it gave way beneath my heart's full beat
Which tried at an exultant prophecy
But dropped before the measure was complete –
Alas, for songs and hearts! O Tuscany,
O Dante's Florence, is the type too plain?
Didst thou, too, only sing of liberty

As little children take up a high strain
With unintentioned voices, and break off
To sleep upon their mothers' knees again?
Could'st thou not watch one hour? then, sleep enough
– That sleep may hasten manhood and sustain
The faint pale spirit with some muscular stuff.

***

From Casa Guidi windows I looked forth,
And saw ten thousand eyes of Florentines
Flash back the triumph of the Lombard north, –
Saw fifty banners, freighted with the signs
And exultations of the awakened earth,
Float on above the multitude in lines,
Straight to the Pitti. So, the vision went.
And so, between those populous rough hands
Raised in the sun, Duke Leopold outleant,
And took the patriot's oath which henceforth stands
Among the oaths of perjurers, eminent
To catch the lightnings ripened for these lands.

***

✺✺✺ Critique: 'Casa Guidi Windows'

Separated in two parts, the first has twenty stanzas, and the second has fifteen; they were published respectively in 1848 and 1850. Browning composed her stanzas looking from the now iconic Casa Guidi in Florence where she made a home with Robert Browning.

Windows here are a profound metaphor for the way in which the poet uses her disconnection from the culture and its streets to help petiton for Italy's unification movement, known as the Risorgimento. She literally has a bird's-eye view of this battle for Italy's liberty, writing the events as they happen. Like a composer might a score, she writes music of the revolution from her quiet room for the ears of the European establishment. In this case, the unheard songs are from the street below not her imagination. By Part II, it dawns on her that without the support of the rest of Europe the Italians will not win; the poem contains a roll call of names of those who might help the cause, like Napolean III "my hero".

"O bella Liberta," the famous phrase here sung by a child, encapsulates the aspiration for liberty and catapults the beginning of the poem straight into the fight for Italy. By setting childlike purity against the backdrop of political struggle she shows that freedom is transcendent, a fundamental desire for child and beasts; the fight for liberty is a part of nature, the song of the eternal.

From her windows, she frames the songs highlighting the cultural and historical context of Florence, a city steeped in its fight for liberty, even since Dante. The imagery of the child "stringing" the words, the vitality and energy of revolution, the very act of singing is the heartbeat of Italy past and future. Barrett Browning's image of the trembling bush from which the bird flies reflects the nature of the pursuit of freedom.

In Part II, the child's song is now likened to an "exultant prophecy" that ultimately falters, suggesting the fragility of dreams in the face of reality, a fragility that she feels herself physically "the faint pale spirit, with some muscular stuff" is at once what she observes outside and what she feels physically herself, always fighting for her independence from the enemy of her sickness.

Towards the end of 1859, the achievement of unity seems to be approaching, and Barrett Browning becomes so enthusiastic that she leaves this window view and takes to the streets with the patriots, a gesture that will cost a fair amount of damage to her fragile health. The initial trust placed in Napoleon III will collapse with the signing of the Peace of Villa Franca, generating a deep wound that will compromise this heroine of the Italian cause, both psychologically and physically.

First News from Villafranca

Peace, peace, peace, do you say?
What! – with the enemy's guns in our ears?
With the country's wrong not rendered back?
What! – while Austria stands at bay
In Mantua, and our Venice bears
The cursed flag of the yellow and black?

Peace, peace, peace, do you say?
And this the Mincio? Where's the fleet,
And where's the sea? Are we all blind
Or mad with the blood shed yesterday,
Ignoring Italy under our feet,
And seeing things before, behind?

Peace, peace, peace, do you say?
What! – uncontested, undenied?
Because we triumph, we succumb?
A pair of Emperors stand in the way
(One of whom is a man, beside),
To sign and seal our cannons dumb?

No, not Napoleon! – he who mused
At Paris, and at Milan spake,
And at Solferino led the fight:
Not he we trusted, honoured, used
Our hopes and hearts for ... till they break
Even so, you tell us ... in his sight.

Peace, peace, is still your word?
We say you lie then! – that is plain,
There is no peace, and shall be none.
Our very Dead would cry "Absurd!"
And clamor that they died in vain,
And whine to come back to the sun.

Hush! more reverence for the Dead!
They've done the most for Italy
Evermore since the earth was fair.
Now would that we had died instead,
Still dreaming peace meant liberty,
And did not, could not, mean despair.

Peace, you say? – yes, peace, in truth!
But such a peace as the ear can achieve
'Twixt the rifle's click and the rush of the ball,
'Twixt the tiger's spring and the crunch of the tooth,
'Twixt the dying atheist's negative
And God's Face – waiting, after all!

The Forced Recruit (*Extract*)

In the ranks of the Austrian you found him,
He died with his face to you all;
Yet bury him here where around him
You honour your bravest that fall.

Venetian, fair – featured and slender,
He lies shot to death in his youth,
With a smile on his lips over-tender
For any mere soldier's dead mouth.

No stranger, and yet not a traitor,
Though alien the cloth on his breast,
Underneath it how seldom a greater
Young heart, has a shot sent to rest!

By your enemy tortured and goaded
To march with them, stand in their file,
His musket (see) never was loaded,
He facing your guns with that smile!

As orphans yearn on to their mothers,
He yearned to your patriot bands; –
"Let me die for our Italy, brothers,
If not in your ranks, by your hands!"

"Aim straightly, fire steadily! spare me
A ball in the body which may
Deliver my heart here, and tear me
This badge of the Austrian away!"

***

Mother and Poet (*Extract*)

Dead! One of them shot by the sea in the east,
And one of them shot in the west by the sea.
Dead! both my boys! When you sit at the feast
And are wanting a great song for Italy free,
Let none look at *me*!

Yet I was a poetess only last year,
And good at my art, for a woman, men said;
But *this* woman, *this*, who is agonized here,
– The east sea and west sea rhyme on in her head
For ever instead.

What art can a woman be good at? Oh, vain!
What art *is* she good at, but hurting her breast
With the milk–teeth of babes, and a smile at the pain?
Ah boys, how you hurt! you were strong as you pressed,
And I proud, by that test.

***

Are souls straight so happy that, dizzy with Heaven,
They drop earth's affections, conceive not of woe?
I think not. Themselves were too lately forgiven
Through THAT Love and Sorrow which reconciled so
The Above and Below.

O Christ of the five wounds, who look'dst through the dark
To the face of Thy mother! consider, I pray,
How we common mothers stand desolate, mark,
Whose sons, not being Christs, die with eyes turned away,
And no last word to say!

Both boys dead? but that's out of nature. We all
Have been patriots, yet each house must always keep one.
'Twere imbecile, hewing out roads to a wall;
And, when Italy 's made, for what end is it done
If we have not a son?

The North and the South

I

"Now give us lands where the olives grow,"
Cried the North to the South,
"Where the sun with a golden mouth can blow
Blow bubbles of grapes down a vineyard–row!"
Cried the North to the South.

"Now give us men from the sunless plain,"
Cried the South to the North,
"By need of work in the snow and rain,
Made strong, and brave by familiar pain!"
Cried the South to the North.

II

"Give lucider hills and intenser seas,"
Said the North to the South.
"Since ever by symbols and bright degrees
Art, childlike, climbs to the dear Lord's knees,"
Said the North to the South.

"Give strenuous souls for belief and prayer",
Said the South to the North,
"That stand in the dark on the lowest stair,
While affirming of God 'He is certainly there,'"
Said the South to the North.

III

"Yet oh, for the skies that are softer and higher!"
Sighed the North to the South;
"For the flowers that blaze, and the trees that aspire,
And the insects made of a song or a fire!"
Sighed the North to the South.

"And oh, for a seer to discern the same!"
Sighed the South to the North;
"For a poet's tongue of baptismal flame,
To call the tree or the flower by its name!"
Sighed the South to the North.

IV

The North sent therefore a man of men,
As a grace to the South;
And thus to Rome came Andersen.
"Alas, but must you take him again?"
Said the South to the North

Napoleon III in Italy (*Extract*)

***

Great is he
Who uses his greatness for all.
His name shall stand perpetually
As a name to applaud and cherish,
Not only within the civic wall
For the loyal, but also without
For the generous and free.
Just is he,
Who is just for the popular due
As well as the private debt.
The praise of nations ready to perish
Fall on him, – crown him in view
Of tyrants caught in the net,
And statesmen dizzy with fear and doubt!
And though, because they are many,
And he is merely one,
And nations selfish and cruel
Heap up the inquisitor's fuel
To kill the body of high intents,
And burn great deeds from their place,
Till this, the greatest of any,

May seem imperfectly done;
Courage, whoever circumvents!
Courage, courage, whoever is base!
The soul of a high intent, be it known,
Can die no more than any soul
Which God keeps by Him under the throne;
And this, at whatever interim,
Shall live, and be consummated
Into the being of deeds made whole.
Courage, courage! happy is he,
Of whom (himself among the dead
And silent) this word shall be said:
– That he might have had the world with him,
But chose to side with suffering men,
And had the world against him when
He came to deliver Italy.
Emperor
Evermore.

Christmas Gifts (*Extract*)

The Pope on Christmas Day
Sits in Saint Peter's chair;
But the peoples murmur and say
"Our souls are sick and forlorn,
And who will show us where
Is the stable where Christ was born?"

The star is lost in the dark;
The manger is lost in the straw,
The Christ cries faintly ... hark! ...
Through bands that swaddle and strangle –
But the Pope in the chair of awe
Looks down the great quadrangle.

***

Italy and the World (*Extract*)

***

I cry aloud in my poet-passion,
Viewing my England o'er Alp and sea.
I loved her more in her ancient fashion:
She carries her rifles too thick for me
Who spares them so in the cause of a brother.

Suspicion, panic? end this pother.
The sword, kept sheathless at peacetime, rusts.
None fears for himself while he feels for another:
The brave man either fights or trusts,
And wears no mail in his private chamber.

Beautiful Italy! golden amber
Warm with the kisses of lover and traitor!
Thou who hast drawn us on to remember,
Draw us to hope now: let us be greater
By this new future than that old story.

Chapter Four: Women's Rights & Feminism

The feminist works of Barrett Browning challenge traditional gender roles and advocate for women's intellectual and emotional autonomy.

In the early years of her womanhood, Elizabeth didn't hold a traditional place in society, or indeed within her household. She was born wealthy and even though her mother's death made her the eldest female at twenty-two, she was not well enough to help as a homemaker or bring home money for the family.

In such poems as 'Work and Contemplation' and 'A Year's Spinning', she depicts the life of a typical working woman of her generation as sad, laborious and lamentable. For Barrett Browning, working meant writing and publishing – a female career distinctly undervalued in Victorian England. Even though she never truly received the recognition she deserved in her lifetime, art gave her a means self-expression and, crucially, independence.

Anger seeps through Elizabeth's poems, where beautiful bird-like women, central to the majority of her narratives, experience great suffering. At the time, marriage was often a woman's best chance of improving her circumstances, so poems like 'A Lady's Yes' challenged their agency over major life choices. Tragically, infant mortality was also high, which was poignantly portrayed in pieces like 'Isobel's Child'. This kind of hardship, Elizabeth argued, was always underpinned by the expectation in society that women should smile through their grief, as she cleverly penned in 'The Mask'.

Repeatedly, a woman's looks – fine dresses, beauty and fair curls – are used as a tool to suggest that appearance was valued more highly than intellect. In 'A Court Lady', the nurse carefully fixes her looks before starting her important medical work. Again, in 'Lord Walter's Wife', the speaker is so angered by a "fair" lady with "ugly": words that he refuses to speak to her. The outspoken Elizabeth was a woman determined to be heard, and not just seen.

The Romaunt of Margret (*Extract*)

***

The lady did not heed
That the far stars did fail;
Still calm her smile, albeit the while...
Nay, but she is not pale!
"I have more than a friend
Across the mountains dim:
No other's voice is soft to me,
Unless it nameth him."
Margret, Margret.

***

"He loved but only thee!
That love is transient too.
The wild hawk's bill doth dabble still
I' the mouth that vowed thee true:
Will he open his dull eyes
When tears fall on his brow?
Behold, the death-worm to his heart
Is a nearer thing than thou,
Margret, Margret."

Her face was on the ground –
None saw the agony;
But the men at sea did that night agree
They heard a drowning cry:
And when the morning brake,
Fast rolled the river's tide,
With the green trees waving overhead
And a white corse laid beside.
Margret, Margret.

Aurora Leigh: Book I (*Extract*)

***

She had lived
A sort of cage-bird life, born in a cage,
Accounting that to leap from perch to perch
Was act and joy enough for any bird.
Dear heaven, how silly are the things that live
In thickets, and eat berries!

I, alas,
A wild bird scarcely fledged, was brought to her cage,
And she was there to meet me. Very kind.
Bring the clean water; give out the fresh seed.

***

Aurora Leigh: Book III

(*Extract*)

***

Leave the lamp, Susan, and go up to bed.
The room does very well; I have to write
Beyond the stroke of midnight. Get away;
Your steps, for ever buzzing in the room,
Tease me like gnats. Ah, letters! throw them down
At once, as I must have them, to be sure,
Whether I bid you never bring me such
At such an hour, or bid you. No excuse;
You choose to bring them, as I choose perhaps
To throw them in the fire. Now get to bed,
And dream, if possible, I am not cross.

Why what a pettish, petty thing I grow, –
A mere mere woman, a mere flaccid nerve,
A kerchief left out all night in the rain,
Turned soft so, – overtasked and overstrained
And overlived in this close London life!
And yet I should be stronger.

Never burn
Your letters, poor Aurora! for they stare
With red seals from the table, saying each,
"Here's something that you know not."

***

✸✸✸ Critique: 'Aurora Leigh: Book III'

During her three years away from Romney, with whom she will reunite in Book VI, Aurora has gained poetic renown and receives many letters from admirers, though none are from Romney, who is doubtful of her poetic pursuits. She is currently working as a bookseller and writing for various publications to support herself, so these lines perhaps exemplify best the nature of the poem's autobiography: this is Elizabeth speaking directly to us as Aurora speaking to Susan.

In Book III, the poet wants to express clearly the way in which women can feel buried alive by societal constraints, and their resurrection, along with a transformation of society, can be achieved through a poetic vision akin to spiritual enlightenment.

The image of a dark claustrophobic room illuminated by a lamp, symbolizes the "seer" enlightened by poetry. This illumination reveals Aurora's spiritual nature while highlighting the challenges she faces as a poet compelled to write in the solitude of night. The room is filled with the emotional fire of her creative spirit, yet she struggles with the intrusions that hinder her writing, distracted by the letters and sounds around her, she speaks out.

The influence of George Eliot and John Ruskin are palpable throughout the work where the design often precedes the plot: "my chief intention is the writing of a novel-poem." Her challenge to the novelists of her time, a turf war in which she is reclaiming the ground of storytelling and social commentary for poetry.

She employs the colloquial and conversational tone reminiscent of George Eliot, of whom she was a great admirer (Eliot was a novelist who took a man's name for different reasons to George Sand.)

This passage emphasizes that carving out a space for writing is no simple endeavour. The writing process often leaves writers irritable and insecure, plagued by self-doubt: "why what a pettish petty thing I grow ... a mere, mere woman ... a mere flaccid nerve ... overlived in this close London life."

Ultimately, the letters symbolize the unknown and the outside world and opportunities that lie beyond her dark, narrow understanding of what it means to be a true poet, and encourage us to read on.

To George Sand: A Recognition

True genius, but true woman! dost deny
The woman's nature with a manly scorn
And break away the gauds and armlets worn
By weaker women in captivity?
Ah, vain denial! that revolted cry
Is sobbed in by a woman's voice forlorn –
Thy woman's hair, my sister, all unshorn
Floats back dishevelled strength in agony
Disproving thy man's name: and while before
The world thou burnest in a poet-fire,
We see thy woman-heart beat evermore
Through the large flame. Beat purer, heart, and higher,
Till God unsex thee on the heavenly shore
Where unincarnate spirits purely aspire!

Work and Contemplation

The woman singeth at her spinning–wheel
A pleasant chant, ballad or barcarole;
She thinketh of her song, upon the whole,
Far more than of her flax; and yet the reel
Is full, and artfully her fingers feel
With quick adjustment, provident control,
The lines, too subtly twisted to unroll
Out to a perfect thread. I hence appeal
To the dear Christian Church, that we may do
Our Father's business in these temples mirk,
Thus swift and steadfast, thus intent and strong;
While thus, apart from toil, our souls pursue
Some high calm spheric tune, and prove our work
The better for the sweetness of our song.

A Year's Spinning

He listened at the porch that day,
To hear the wheel go on, and on;
And then it stopped, ran back away,
While through the door he brought the sun:
But now my spinning is all done.

He sat beside me, with an oath
That love ne'er ended, once begun;
I smiled – believing for us both,
What was the truth for only one:
And now my spinning is all done.

My mother cursed me that I heard
A young man's wooing as I spun:
Thanks, cruel mother, for that word –
For I have, since, a harder known!
And now my spinning is all done.

I thought – God! – my first-born's cry
Both voices to mine ear would drown:
I listened in mine agony –
It was the silence made me groan!
And now my spinning is all done.

Bury me 'twixt my mother's grave,
(Who cursed me on her death-bed lone)
And my dead baby's (God it save!)
Who, not to bless me, would not moan.
And now my spinning is all done.

A stone upon my heart and head,
But no name written on the stone!
Sweet neighbours, whisper low instead,
"This sinner was a loving one –
And now her spinning is all done."

And let the door ajar remain,
In case he should pass by anon;
And leave the wheel out very plain, –
That HE, when passing in the sun,
May see the spinning is all done.

A Woman's Shortcomings

She has laughed as softly as if she sighed,
She has counted six, and over,
Of a purse well filled, and a heart well tried –
Oh, each a worthy lover!
They "give her time"; for her soul must slip
Where the world has set the grooving;
She will lie to none with her fair red lip –
But love seeks truer loving.

She trembles her fan in a sweetness dumb,
As her thoughts were beyond recalling;
With a glance for one, and a glance for some,
From her eyelids rising and falling;
Speaks common words with a blushful air,
Hears bold words, unreproving;
But her silence says – what she never will swear – And
love seeks better loving.

Go, lady! lean to the night-guitar,
And drop a smile to the bringer;
Then smile as sweetly, when he is far,
At the voice of an in-door singer.
Bask tenderly beneath tender eyes;
Glance lightly, on their removing;
And join new vows to old perjuries –
But dare not call it loving!

Unless you can think, when the song is done,
No other is soft in the rhythm;
Unless you can feel, when left by One,
That all men else go with him;
Unless you can know, when unpraised by his breath,
That your beauty itself wants proving;
Unless you can swear "For life, for death!" –
Oh, fear to call it loving!

Unless you can muse in a crowd all day
On the absent face that fixed you;
Unless you can love, as the angels may,
With the breadth of heaven betwixt you;
Unless you can dream that his faith is fast,
Through behoving and unbehoving;
Unless you can die when the dream is past, –
Oh, never call it loving!

The Lady's Yes

"Yes!" I answered you last night;
"No!" this morning, Sir, I say!
Colours, seen by candle-light,
Will not look the same by day.

When the tabors played their best,
Lamps above, and laughs below –
Love me sounded like a jest,
Fit for *Yes* or fit for *No*!

Call me false, or call me free –
Vow, whatever light may shine,
No man on your face shall see
Any grief for change on mine.

Yet the sin is on us both –
Time to dance is not to woo –
Wooer light makes fickle troth –
Scorn of *me* recoils on *you*!

Learn to win a lady's faith
Nobly, as the thing is high;
Bravely, as for life and death –
With a loyal gravity.

Lead her from the festive boards,
Point her to the starry skies,
Guard her, by your truthful words,
Pure from courtship's flatteries.

By your truth she shall be true –
Ever true, as wives of yore –
And her *Yes*, once said to you,
SHALL be Yes for evermore.

Void in Law

Sleep, little babe, on my knee,
Sleep, for the midnight is chill,
And the moon has died out in the tree,
And the great human world goeth ill.
Sleep, for the wicked agree:
Sleep, let them do as they will.
Sleep.

Sleep, thou hast drawn from my breast
The last drop of milk that was good;
And now, in a dream, suck the rest,
Lest the real should trouble thy blood.
Suck, little lips dispossessed,
As we kiss in the air whom we would.
Sleep.

O lips of thy father! the same,
So like! Very deeply they swore
When he gave me his ring and his name,
To take back, I imagined, no more!
And now is all changed like a game,
Though the old cards are used as of yore?
Sleep.

"Void in law," said the Courts. Something wrong
In the forms? Yet, "Till death part us two,
I, James, take thee, Jessie," was strong,
And ONE witness competent. True
Such a marriage was worth an old song,
Heard in Heaven though, as plain as the New.
Sleep.

Sleep, little child, his and mine!
Her throat has the antelope curve,
And her cheek just the color and line
Which fade not before him nor swerve:
Yet she has no child! – the divine
Seal of right upon loves that deserve.
Sleep.

My child! though the world take her part,
Saying "She was the woman to choose,
He had eyes, was a man in his heart," –
We twain the decision refuse:
We ... weak as I am, as thou art...
Cling on to him, never to loose.
Sleep.

***

Lady Geraldine's Courtship (*Extract*)

***

He had left her, peradventure, when my footstep proved
my coming,
But for *her* – he half arose, then sate, grew scarlet and grew pale.
Oh, she trembled! 't is so always with a worldly man or woman
In the presence of true spirits; what else *can* they do but quail?

Oh, she fluttered like a tame bird, in among its forest-brothers
Far too strong for it; then drooping, bowed her face upon her
hands;
And I spake out wildly, fiercely, brutal truths of her and others:
I, she planted in the desert, swathed her, windlike, with my sands.

I plucked up her social fictions, bloody-rooted though
leaf-verdant,
Trod them down with words of shaming, – all the purple and
the gold.
All the "landed stakes" and lordships, all that spirits pure
and ardent
Are cast out of love and honour because chancing not to hold.

"For myself I do not argue," said I, "though I love you, madam,
But for better souls that nearer to the height of yours have trod:
And this age shows, to my thinking, still more infidels to Adam
Than directly, by profession, simple infidels to God.

"Yet, O God," I said, "O grave," I said, "O mother's heart
and bosom,
With whom first and last are equal, saint and corpse and
little child!
We are fools to your deductions, in these figments of
heart-closing;
We are traitors to your causes, in these sympathies defiled.

"Learn more reverence, madam, not for rank or wealth –
that needs no learning:
That comes quickly, quick as sin does, ay, and culminates to sin;
But for Adam's seed, MAN! Trust me, 't is a clay above your
scorning,

With God's image stamped upon it, and God's kindling
breath within.
"What right have you, madam, gazing in your palace mirror daily,
Getting so by heart your beauty which all others must adore,
While you draw the golden ringlets down your fingers, to vow gaily
You will wed no man that's only good to God, and nothing more?

To George Sand: A Desire

Thou large-brained woman and large-hearted man,
Self-called George Sand! whose soul, amid the lions
Of thy tumultuous senses, moans defiance
And answers roar for roar, as spirits can:
I would some mild miraculous thunder ran
Above the applauded circus, in appliance
Of thine own nobler nature's strength and science,
Drawing two pinions, white as wings of swan,
From thy strong shoulders, to amaze the place
With holier light! that thou to woman's claim
And man's, mightst join beside the angel's grace
Of a pure genius sanctified from blame
Till child and maiden pressed to thine embrace
To kiss upon thy lips a stainless fame.

✷✷✷ Critique: 'To George Sand: A Desire'

One of a sonnet pair – the other is 'To George Sand: A Recognition' – and a part of the collection *Poems* published in 1844 after Barrett Browning had returned grief-stricken to Wimpole Street from Torquay, this poem represents a more sophisticated understanding of the sonnet form's potential. She had not yet met Robert Browning and was still coping with the trauma of family death.

'George Sand', a name invented by the subject of the poem, Amantine Lucile Aurore Dupin, was the great cross-dressing novelist of the European Romantic period. Under her assumed male pseudonym she denounced marriage and was the long-time lover of Chopin. In her time more famous than Victor Hugo and Honoré de Balzac, she liberated the female heroines of her novels from the constraints of societal norms.

Wordplay is the repeating theme of the poem: "desire" doesn't mean to lust after but to aspire to and revere. EBB uses the form as a document not a romance; she is creating a phraseology to celebrate the way in which Sand has designed a woman for the times. The subject's diverse qualities are laid out side by side with concision and immediacy as one might arrange significant objects in a portrait.

The poem begins with a roar and ends with a kiss. It is brimming with diverse associations and historical tropes, all neatly controlled by the form: the name Plato, helps her lionize Sand. And the central image "amid the lions" in a circus alludes perhaps to controversial figures with notoriety and facing cancellation. Each contrasting image is woven with its opposite along the lines: "That thou to woman's claim / And man's, mightest join beside the angel's grace / Of a pure genius..."

This recalibration is a skillful ornament, strength and sensitivity are given equal voice and space. The separate territories of serenity and power are beginning to align in European society, and with this sonnet Elizabeth shows herself to be very much part of the movement, drawing "white as wings of swan, / From thy strong shoulders". She has constructed writer and subject as a dual power stepping fearlessly into a man's world.

My Kate

She was not as pretty as women I know,
And yet all your best made of sunshine and snow
Drop to shade, melt to nought in the long-trodden ways,
While she's still remembered on warm and cold days –
My Kate.

Her air had a meaning, her movements a grace;
You turned from the fairest to gaze on her face;
And when you had once seen her forehead and mouth,
You saw as distinctly her soul and her truth –
My Kate.

Such a blue inner light from her eyelids outbroke,
You looked at her silence and fancied she spoke;
When she did, so peculiar yet soft was the tone,
Though the loudest spoke also, you heard her alone –
My Kate.

I doubt if she said to you much that could act
As a thought or suggestion; she did not attract
In the sense of the brilliant or wise; I infer
'Twas her thinking of others made you think of her –
My Kate.

She never found fault with you, never implied
Your wrong by her right; and yet men at her side
Grew nobler, girls purer, as through the whole town
The children were gladder that pulled at her gown –
My Kate.

None knelt at her feet confessed lovers in thrall;
They knelt more to God than they used – that was all;
If you praised her as charming, some asked what you meant,
But the charm of her presence was felt when she went –
My Kate.

The weak and the gentle, the ribald and rude,
She took as she found them, and did them all good;
It always was so with her – see what you have!
She has made the grass greener even here with her grave –

The Romaunt of the Page

(*Extract*)

***

The page stopped weeping and smiled cold –
"Your wisdom may declare
That womanhood is proved the best
By golden brooch and glossy vest
The mincing ladies wear;
Yet is it proved, and was of old,
Anear as well, I dare to hold,
By truth, or by despair."

He smiled no more, he wept no more,
But passionate he spake –
"Oh, womanly she prayed in tent,
When none beside did wake!
Oh, womanly she paled in fight,
For one belovèd's sake
And her little hand, defiled with blood,
Her tender tears of womanhood
Most woman-pure did make!"

– "Well done it were for thy sister,
Thou tellest well her tale!
But for my lady, she shall pray
I' the kirk of Nydesdale.
Not dread for me but love for me
Shall make my lady pale;
No casque shall hide her woman's tear –
It shall have room to trickle clear
Behind her woman's veil."

"But what if she mistook thy mind
And followed thee to strife,
Then kneeling did entreat thy love
As Paynims ask for life?"
– "I would forgive, and evermore
Would love her as my servitor,
But little as my wife.

Bertha in the Lane (*Extract*)

***

Colder grow my hands and feet.
When I wear the shroud I made,
Let the folds lie straight and neat,
And the rosemary be spread,
That if any friend should come,
(To see thee, Sweet!) all the room
May be lifted out of gloom.

And, dear Bertha, let me keep
On my hand this little ring,
Which at nights, when others sleep,
I can still see glittering!
Let me wear it out of sight,
In the grave, – where it will light
All the dark up, day and night.

On that grave drop not a tear!
Else, though fathom-deep the place,
Through the woollen shroud I wear
I shall feel it on my face.
Rather smile there, blessèd one,
Thinking of me in the sun,
Or forget me – smiling on!

Art thou near me? nearer! so –
Kiss me close upon the eyes,
That the earthly light may go
Sweetly, as it used to rise
When I watched the morning-gray
Strike, betwixt the hills, the way
He was sure to come that day.

So, – no more vain words be said!
The hosannas nearer roll.
Mother, smile now on thy Dead,
I am death-strong in my soul.
Mystic Dove alit on cross,
Guide the poor bird of the snows
Through the snow-wind above loss!

Jesus, Victim, comprehending
Love's divine self-abnegation,
Cleanse my love in its self-spending,
And absorb the poor libation!
Wind my thread of life up higher,
Up, through angels' hands of fire!
I aspire while I expire.

Lord Walter's Wife (*Extract*)

"But where do you go?" said the lady, while both sat under the yew,
And her eyes were alive in their depth, as the kraken beneath the sea-blue.

"Because I fear you," he answered; "because you are far too fair,
And able to strangle my soul in a mesh of your gold-coloured hair."

"Oh that," she said, "is no reason! Such knots are quickly undone,
And too much beauty, I reckon, is nothing but too much sun."

"Yet farewell so," he answered; "the sunstroke's fatal at times.
I value your husband, Lord Walter, whose gallop rings still from the limes."

"Oh that," she said, "is no reason. You smell a rose
through a fence:
If two should smell it what matter? who grumbles,
and where's the pretense?"

"But I," he replied, "have promised another, when
love was free,
To love her alone, alone, who alone from afar loves
me."

"Why, that," she said, "is no reason. Love's always
free I am told.
Will you vow to be safe from the headache on
Tuesday, and think it will hold?"

***

At which he rose up in his anger, "Why now, you no
longer are fair!
Why, now, you no longer are fatal, but ugly and
hateful, I swear."

At which she laughed out in her scorn: "These men!
Oh these men overnice,
Who are shocked if a colour not virtuous is frankly
put on by a vice."

***

Isobel's Child (*Extract*)

To rest the weary nurse has gone:
An eight-day watch had watched she,
Still rocking beneath sun and moon
The baby on her knee,
Till Isobel its mother said
"The fever waneth – wend to bed,
For now the watch comes round to me."

Then wearily the nurse did throw
Her pallet in the darkest place
Of that sick room, and slept and dreamed:
For, as the gusty wind did blow
The night-lamp's flare across her face,
She saw or seemed to see, but dreamed,
That the poplars tall on the opposite hill
The seven tall poplars on the hill,
Did clasp the setting sun until
His rays dropped from him, pined and still
As blossoms in frost,
Till he waned and paled, so weirdly crossed,
To the colour of moonlight which doth pass
Over the dank ridged churchyard grass.
The poplars held the sun, and he
The eyes of the nurse that they should not see

– Not for a moment, the babe on her knee,
Though she shuddered to feel that it grew to be
Too chill, and lay too heavily.

***

The nurse awakes in the morning sun,
And starts to see beside her bed
The lady with a grandeur spread
Like pathos o'er her face, as one
God-satisfied and earth-undone;
The babe upon her arm was dead:
And the nurse could utter forth no cry, –
She was awed by the calm in the mother's eye.

The Mask (*Extract*)

I have a smiling face, she said,
I have a jest for all I meet,
I have a garland for my head
And all its flowers are sweet, –
And so you call me gay, she said.

Grief taught to me this smile, she said,
And Wrong did teach this jesting bold;
These flowers were plucked from gardenbed
While a death-chime was tolled:
And what now will you say? – she said.

Behind no prison-grate, she said,
Which slurs the sunshine half a mile,
Live captives so uncomforted
As souls behind a smile.
God's pity let us pray, she said.

I know my face is bright, she said, –
Such brightness dying suns diffuse:
I bear upon my forehead shed
The sign of what I lose,
The ending of my day, she said.

If I dared leave this smile, she said,
And take a moan upon my mouth,
And tie a cypress round my head,
And let my tears run smooth,
It were the happier way, she said.

And since that must not be, she said,
I fain your bitter world would leave.
How calmly, calmly smile the Dead,
Who do not, therefore, grieve!
The yea of Heaven is yea, she said.

***

Bianca among the Nightingales (*Extract*)

***

Too bold to sin, too weak to die;
Such women are so. As for me,
I would we had drowned there, he and I,
That moment, loving perfectly.
He had not caught her with her loosed
Gold ringlets ... rarer in the south ...
Nor heard the "Grazie tanto" bruised
To sweetness by her English mouth.
And still they sing, the nightingales.

She had not reached him at my heart
With her fine tongue, as snakes indeed
**** flies; nor had I, for my part,
Yearned after, in my desperate need,
And followed him as he did her
To coasts left bitter by the tide,
Whose very nightingales, elsewhere
Delighting, torture and deride!
For still they sing, the nightingales.

A worthless woman! mere cold clay
As all false things are! but so fair,
She takes the breath of men away
Who gaze upon her unaware.
I would not play her larcenous tricks
To have her looks! She lied and stole,
And spat into my love's pure pyx
The rank saliva of her soul.
And still they sing, the nightingales.

***

The Poet and the Bird (*Extract*)

Said a people to a poet "Go out from among us
straightway!
While we are thinking earthly things, thou singest of
divine.
There's a little fair brown nightingale, who, sitting in
the gateways
Makes fitter music to our ears than any song of thine!"

***

A Court Lady (*Extract*)

Her hair was tawny with gold, her eyes with purple
   were dark,
Her cheeks' pale opal burnt with a red and restless
   spark.

Never was lady of Milan nobler in name and in race;
Never was lady of Italy fairer to see in the face.

Never was lady on earth more true as woman and wife,
Larger in judgment and instinct, prouder in manners
   and life.

She stood in the early morning, and said to her
   maidens, "Bring
That silken robe made ready to wear at the court of
   the king.

"Bring me the clasps of diamond, lucid, clear of the
 mote,
Clasp me the large at the waist, and clasp me the
 small at the throat.

"Diamonds to fasten the hair, and diamonds to fasten
 the sleeves,
Laces to drop from their rays, like a powder of snow
 from the eaves."

Gorgeous she entered the sunlight which gathered her
 up in a flame,
While, straight in her open carriage, she to the
 hospital came.

***

Acknowledgements

Pelé Cox would like to thank Suzi Feay and special thanks to Fabio Barry.

The publishers would like to thank Alamy Images/Pictorial Press Ltd for the image of Elizabeth Barrett Browning on page 6, and Lou Benesch at loubenesch.com for her inspired cover illustration.

Bibliography & Further Reading

Barrett Browning, Elizabeth; *Sonnets from the Portuguese and Other Poems*; Dover Books, 2000.

Barrett Browning, Elizabeth; *The Complete Poems of Elizabeth Barrett Browning*, Legare Street Press, 2022.

Bolton, John, and Holloway, Julia, eds; *Aurora Leigh and Other Poems*, Penguin Classics, 1995.

Foster Margaret; *Elizabeth Barrett Browning: A Biography*, Doubleday, 1989.

Sampson, Fiona; *Two Way Mirror: The Life of Elizabeth Barrett Browning*, Profile Books, 2021.

Stack, V.E., ed; *The Love Letters of Robert Browning and Elizabeth Barrett*, Random House, 1987.